D1759685

TUDOR MONARCHS

VIVE·LE·NOBLE·ROY·HENRY

TUDOR MONARCHS
Lives in Letters

Andrea Clarke

BRITISH LIBRARY

For Sophie Holmes, Juliet Malbon & Arabella Harding, three little princesses.

First published in 2017 by
The British Library
96 Euston Road
London NW1 2DB

Cataloguing in Publication Data
A catalogue record for this publication is available
from The British Library

ISBN 978 07123 5774 6
Introduction © Andrea Clarke 2017
Text compilation and editorial © Andrea Clarke 2017
All images copyright © the British Library Board
Designed and typeset by Briony Hartley, Goldust Design
Printed in China by C&C Offset Printing Co., Ltd

p. 2: Henry VII's coat of arms, from British Library Royal 19 B.xvi, f.1v.

p. 6: Detail from British Library, Egerton MS 616, f. 14.

p. 48: Engraving of Henry VIII from a painting in the Royal Gallery at Kensington. Set of engravings of 'the heads of the Kings of England' by George Vertue, 1736. 191.g.9.

p. 116: Engraving of Edward VI from an original in Kensington Palace. Set of engravings of 'the heads of the Kings of England' by George Vertue, 1736. 191.g.9.

p. 146: Engraving of Mary I from a picture in possession of the Rt Hon the Earl of Oxford. Set of engravings of 'the heads of the Kings of England' by George Vertue, 1736. 191.g.9.

p. 162: Engraving of Elizabeth I from Henry Holland, *a Booke of Kings; beeing the true and likely Effigies of all our English Kings from the Conquest ... untill this present. With their severall Coats of Armes, Impreses and Devises ... graven in copper, etc.*, 1618. C.38.g.3.

Contents

...a procrastinatio v̄ri ad me adu...
...q̄ huic meo tā ardenti in se an...
...oro vt cepit / et sicuti ego sui n...
...uoq̄ et ipsa meū recens nomē in...
...ū maturet: vt ex absentib; sring p...
...erata gaudia suos aliquado fru...
...rtas finuixit) sū exorturg in com...
...e parentib; meis / atq̄ in declaran...
...quidem fiut illis p̄ratū audir...
...q̄ obsecro v̄ro quoq̄ Cel.mi nu...
...dere: et Sere.mis Dn̄s meis ūns...
...eos aut nō secus q̄m si mei p...
...or. et obsecuo. atq̄ illis felicia e...
...tas felix et fausta sit. Leta q̄...
...crebro et sepe me uisere velit.

Introduction

In 1485, Henry Tudor, Earl of Richmond, defeated the Yorkist King Richard III at the Battle of Bosworth and, against all the odds, became King Henry VII, England's first Tudor monarch. Emerging from obscurity following fourteen years' exile in France, the new king had asserted his extremely tenuous Lancastrian claim to the English throne, derived by illegitimate descent from his mother Lady Margaret Beaufort, who was the granddaughter of John Beaufort, the eldest son of John of Gaunt, Duke of Lancaster, by his then-mistress, Katherine Swynford. Although the Beaufort line was granted legitimacy in 1397 by Richard II, it was soon excluded from the succession by Henry IV in 1406. On his paternal side, Henry VII's claim to the throne was even weaker: he was descended from Welsh gentry who, although connected by marriage to the Lancastrian King Henry VI, did not have any blood claim to the throne.

From the start, Henry VII's reign was plagued by threats from Yorkist pretenders, rebellions and uprisings. Yet, remarkably, this most unlikely and inexperienced ruler held on to his crown to establish England's famous Tudor dynasty. Henry VII, his son Henry VIII and three grandchildren Edward VI, Mary I and Elizabeth I ruled for just 118 years between them, but in that short period of time they left an indelible mark on English history and a deep and long-lasting impression on posterity. Four centuries on, the turbulent history of Tudor England and its monarchs still continues to intrigue and captivate us. Perhaps this is because, unlike previous ruling dynasties, we feel we know them and can relate to them personally. Thanks to the accuracy of Tudor portraiture, we know what they *really* looked like and can meet them face-to-face, and we can also follow in their footsteps by visiting the magnificent Tudor palaces and stately homes that still dot the English landscape. But, above all, the phenomenal amount of surviving sixteenth-century manuscript material has provided us with a fascinating window into the Tudor period. As a result, we know so much more about the Tudor monarchs than any of their predecessors and it is this that makes them so compelling.

This book presents a narrative account of the Tudor period, told through 42 letters and documents drawn from the British Library's vast collection of Tudor State Papers and historical documents. Each item is reproduced in colour, fully transcribed and accompanied by a commentary to place it in its historical context. Spellings and punctuation have been modernised, and abbreviations and contractions expanded, to make the letters and documents accessible to a wide range of readers. Some of the letters selected from Cotton Library suffered extensive damage in a fire at Ashburnham House in 1731. In such cases, ellipses have been used to indicate lost words. Thankfully, it has sometimes been possible to reconstruct damaged portions of text either by using transcriptions made before 1731 or by employing enhanced imaging techniques. Recovered words are placed within square brackets.

To choose such a small sample of letters and documents from the many thousands held at the British Library was no easy task and so three main criteria were used to make the selection. The first was that each letter had to be either 'autograph', (written in the hand of the author), or at the very least signed by them. Scribal copies of original letters, however interesting, were not considered for inclusion. Other types of documents, if not fully autograph, had to include a significant number of autograph amendments or additions to qualify for inclusion.

The second requirement was that the final selection had to represent as many significant individuals from the Tudor period as possible. Letters written by all the Tudor monarchs are of course included but notes written by Lady Margaret Beaufort and Elizabeth of York also feature, along with letters by Henry VIII's siblings and four of his six wives (unfortunately the British Library does not hold any letters written by Anne of Cleves or Catherine Howard). There are also letters written by Henry VIII's great ministers, Thomas Wolsey, Thomas Cromwell, Thomas More and Thomas Cranmer, as well as William Cecil who stood at the heart of Elizabethan government for 40 years. Letters from the pens of some of those who were executed for treason during the Tudor period, such as Lady Jane Grey, Mary Queen of Scots and the Earl of Essex, can also be found.

The third condition was that each letter or document had to tell a story and either illustrate a key moment in the lives of one of the Tudor monarchs or an important event from their reign. The familiar stories that have enthralled us for centuries are all included: Henry VII and the establishment of the Tudor dynasty, Henry VIII's matrimonial adventures, the break from Rome and the dissolution of the monasteries, the birth of the Church of England and the translation of the Bible into English, the progress of the English Reformation in the reign of Edward VI, the return to Catholicism in the reign of Mary I, the Elizabethan religious settlement, the vexed question of the Elizabeth I's marriage, the execution of Mary, Queen of Scots, the Spanish Armada and the union of the English and Scottish crowns in 1603.

At first glance, these individual sheets of paper can look quite underwhelming, written, as they often are, in indecipherable hands on unadorned paper. But they are in fact jewels beyond price in terms of their historical significance. For, as we turn their pages, we find ourselves transported to a ring-side seat at some of the great moments and events in Tudor history, and we catch fascinating glimpses into the characters and personalities of England's most famous ruling dynasty as they express themselves in their own words.

I am hugely grateful to Jill Purslow, Mary Wellesley and Jill Masterson, each of whom carefully read drafts of the book and provided helpful comments and encouragement. I also wish to thank Laure Miolo for helping me to translate Henry VII's letter to Katherine of Aragon, and Tony Grant for using his photography skills to enable me to decipher the damaged portion of text in Lady Margaret Beaufort's letter to Henry VII.

Andrea Clarke, Lead Curator of
Medieval and Early Modern Manuscripts,
British Library

HENRY VII

Madame I pray you to
membre me / yo^{ur} lovyng
maistre

HENRY R

madame I pray you forget
not me ... to pray to god
that I may ... have ...
your prayers

Elysabeth ...

et moy ie vo^{us} prie ... d angleterre
... en sa ... grace
...

Establishing the Tudor Dynasty

Autograph inscriptions by Henry VII and Elizabeth of York in a fifteenth-century illuminated prayer book.

British Library, Additional MS 17012, f. 21

Madam, I pray you remember me your loving master,
Henry R.

Madam, I pray you forget not me, to pray to God that I may have part of your prayers,
Elizabeth the queen.

Henry Tudor's victory over Richard III at the Battle of Bosworth on 22 August 1485 brought to an end the Wars of the Roses, fought for decades between the feuding houses of York and Lancaster. Henry seized the crown and was proclaimed King Henry VII of England. While still in exile in 1483, Henry had pledged to marry Elizabeth of York, eldest daughter of Edward IV, niece of Richard III and sister of the 'Princes in the Tower'. He realized that Elizabeth's Plantagenet blood and superior hereditary claim to the crown would not only boost the legitimacy of the new Tudor dynasty by shoring up his own weak claim to the throne, but would also help to secure the loyalty of the Yorkists. However, Henry was in no hurry to marry Elizabeth, for he intended to be crowned alone, thereby emphasizing that he was king in his own right, and not dependent upon his wife's dynastic claim. And so, on Sunday 30 October 1485, Henry's coronation took place at Westminster Abbey with great pomp and pageantry. He was surrounded by those who had helped him become king: his uncle Jasper Tudor, whom Henry had rewarded with the dukedom of Bedford; his stepfather Thomas, Lord Stanley, now elevated to the earldom of Derby; John de Vere, Earl of Oxford and fellow-exile in France; and Lady Margaret Beaufort, Henry's mother and most loyal supporter, who is said to have 'wept marvellously' as she witnessed her son crowned the first Tudor monarch.

On 10 December, Sir Thomas Lovell, Speaker of the House of Commons, urged the King to fulfil his promise to marry the 'illustrious Lady Elizabeth, daughter of King Edward IV' to bring about the union of 'two bloods of high renown' and enable 'the propagation of offspring from the stock of kings'. Henry consented and the following day preparations for the royal wedding began and, in a move intended to please the Yorkist faction, Elizabeth, as heiress to her father, was declared Duchess of York. Henry's marriage to Elizabeth took place at Westminster Abbey on 18 January 1486, and their union was symbolized by the Tudor rose – made up of the white rose of the house of York and the red rose adopted by Henry to represent the house of Lancaster. Pope Innocent VIII praised the match, which was also hugely popular with the English people, who hoped that it would bring an end to the civil wars that had afflicted the country in the previous decades and usher in a new era of peace and stability. Although Henry and Elizabeth's marriage was one of political expediency, it was also a love match and produced four children who survived infancy. Arthur, Prince of Wales, their first son and undisputed heir to the English throne, was born in September 1486 and a daughter, named Margaret after Lady Beaufort, 'My Lady the King's Mother', followed in November 1489. With the birth of a second son, Prince Henry (the future Henry VIII), at Greenwich Palace in June 1491, the Tudor succession seemed more than secure. Another daughter was born in March 1496 and named Mary.

Elizabeth of York proved to be a popular and widely admired queen; a Venetian report described her as 'a very handsome woman of great ability and in conduct very able'. Unlike later queens, Elizabeth did not get involved in public affairs or politics and therefore very few letters written by her survive. However, her pious inscriptions and affectionate messages can be found in a number of her favoured servants' prayer books. This Book of Hours belonged to a lady of the court of Henry VII and contains inscriptions by both King Henry and Queen Elizabeth, asking for prayers. In much the same way that people today collect the autographs of famous people, the owner of the prayer book must have been very pleased to obtain these expressions of royal favour.

'My Lady, the King's Mother'

Autograph letter by Lady Margaret Beaufort, to her son Henry VII, expressing her gratitude for his help in the matter of a long-standing debt owed to her by the French crown. Collyweston, 14 January [1501].

This letter was damaged by fire in the Cotton fire of 1731 but it has been possible to recover portions of the text by using enhanced imaging techniques.

British Library, Cotton MS Vespasian F xiii, f. 130r–v

My one sweet and most dear King and all my worldly joy. In as humble manner as I can think, I recommend me to your grace, and most heartily beseech our Lord to bless you. And my good heart, where that ye say that the French King hath at this time given me courteous answer, and written [his] letters of favour to his Court of Parliament, for the true expedition of my matter, which so long hath hanged, the which I well know he doth especially for your sake, for the which my [dear heart I lo]wly beseech your Grace it [may please you] to give him your favourable [letter] of thanks, and to desire him to continue his [valours] in [the sa]me. And, if it so might like your Grace, to do the same to the cardinal, which, as I understand, is your faithful, true and loving servant. I wish my very joy, as I often have showed, and I fortune to get this, or any part thereof, there shall never be that or any good I have, but it shall be yours, and at your commandment, as surely and with as good a will, as any ye have in your coffers; as would God ye could know, it as verily as I think it. But, my dear heart, I will no more encumber your Grace with further writing in this matter, for I am sure your chaplain and servant, Doctor Whitston, hath showed your highness the circumstances of the same; and if it so may like your Grace, I humbly beseech the same, to give further credence also to this bearer. And our Lord give you as long good life, health and joy, as your most noble heart can desire, with as hearty blessings as our Lord hath given me power to give you.

At Colyweston the xiiii day of January, by your faithful true bedewoman, and humble mother.

Margaret R.

17

Lady Margaret Beaufort, founder of the Tudor dynasty in England, was by all accounts a formidable woman. Just thirteen years old and already widowed when she gave birth to Henry Tudor in 1457, Margaret dedicated her life to promoting and protecting her son's interests. It was Margaret's descent from the house of Lancaster that provided Henry with a claim to the English throne, and it was Margaret who advanced his claim, encouraging him to invade England from France in 1485 and providing him with the necessary money and support. Margaret also negotiated Henry's marriage to Elizabeth of York, daughter of Edward IV, in order to secure the English throne for her Tudor son.

Following Henry's victory over Richard III at the Battle of Bosworth in 1485, Margaret was addressed as 'My Lady, the King's Mother' and became the most powerful woman in England. Henry VII demonstrated his gratitude to his devoted mother by restoring her as Countess of Richmond, having her confiscated estates returned to her and making Thomas Stanley – her third husband – the Earl of Derby. Perhaps most remarkable of all, however, was the Act of Parliament that Henry passed which declared Margaret a 'femme sole' or sole person, thereby granting her legal and economic independence from her husband. This enabled Margaret to own property and manage her business affairs, something usually forbidden by common law to married women. As a result, Margaret enjoyed great influence and wealth, which she used to fund several charitable and pious projects. She also became a great patron of learning, founding St John's and Christ's Colleges at Cambridge and chairs of divinity at both Oxford and Cambridge Universities.

Margaret was granted Coldharbour Palace, a fine London residence situated on the banks of the River Thames. This placed her within easy reach of court, where she spent much of her time during Henry's reign, helping to consolidate his position on the throne, guiding him and actively supporting him in his kingship. As the Spanish ambassador observed in 1498, Margaret wielded considerable influence over her son, which did not lessen even after he married Elizabeth of York. In fact, Margaret deliberately cultivated a royal style and shared equal rank with her daughter-in-law in all but title. Contemporary accounts reveal that Margaret frequently accompanied Henry and Elizabeth on royal visits and progresses and that, when the Queen attended important ceremonial occasions, Margaret would accompany her, dressed 'in like mantel and surcoat as the queen, with a rich crownall on her head', or wearing identical 'robes of blood-red cloth furred in white squirrel belly'. Always keen to assert that his mother was just as royal as his Yorkist wife, Henry adopted the Beaufort family's badge of the portcullis as one of the new emblems of English royalty, along with the Tudor and Lancastrian roses. Margaret, in turn, incorporated the royal coronet and fleur-de-lys into her heraldic coat of arms.

Very few of Margaret's letters have survived. This is one of them, addressed to Henry VII and written entirely in her own hand. Margaret expresses her gratitude to her son for the progress he has made with King Louis XII of France in the matter of a substantial, long-standing debt owed to her by the French crown. Although businesslike, the letter also reveals the deep bond that existed between mother and son, for Margaret addresses Henry as 'my dear heart' and 'my one sweet and most dear King and all my worldly joy'. Henry wrote affectionately to his mother too, addressing her as 'my most entirely well beloved Lady and mother'. Margaret's letter also provides further evidence of the regal air that she adopted. After 1499, as here, she signed her letters 'Margaret R'. The 'R' stood for her title, Countess of Richmond, but it could also be read as 'Margaret *Regina*' and no doubt this was an ambiguity that Margaret was happy to encourage.

Margaret died on 29 June 1509. She outlived Henry VII by just two months, but long enough for her to attend the coronation of her grandson Henry VIII and to witness a peaceful succession and the continuation of the Tudor dynasty, which she had fought so hard to establish.

Rival Claimants to the Throne

Letter signed by Perkin Warbeck as 'Your friend Richard of England', to Sir Bernard de la Forsa, requesting his help in securing the support of King Ferdinand II of Aragon. Edinburgh, 18 October 1496.

British Library, Egerton MS 616, f. 6

Right trusty and our right entirely well beloved, we greet you heartily well, signifying unto you that we be credibly informed of the great love, favour and kindness that ye in time past showed unto our most dread lord and father King Edward the fourth, whose soul God rest, with the sage and politic counsels that ye in sundry wises full lovingly gave unto him, whereby he obtained the advancement and promoting of his matters and causes, wherefore ye stood right much in the favour of his Grace. Desire and heartily pray you to be from henceforth unto us as loving faithful and kind counsellor and friend as ye were unto our said father. In showing your good and discreet minds for us in such matters and causes as by your great wisdom, ye shall seem best to be moved for our weal, comfort and relief; and that it will please you to exhort move and stir your lovers and friends to do the same, and that we may understand the good heart and mind that our most dear cousin the King of Spain beareth toward us. And in your so doing, ye may be sure to have us as loving a good lord unto you or better than ever was our said Lord and father. And anything that ye shall of reason desire of us, that may concern the weal of you and of our right trusty and well beloved servant your son Anthony de la Forsa, which hath full lovingly given his long attendance upon us in sundry countries, we shall with good heart be ready to accomplish and perform the same when it shall please Almighty God to send us unto our right in England; and that it may please you to give credence unto your said son of such things as he shall show unto you. And our Lord Jesus preserve you in all honour, joy and felicity, and send you the accomplishment of your noble heart's desire. From Edinburgh in Scotland the xviii day of October.

Your friend Richard of England.

The Wars of the Roses cast dark shadows over England during the early years of Henry VII's reign. Even though Henry's marriage to Elizabeth of York united the two dynasties of York and Lancaster, it did not remove the threat of Yorkist plots against the throne. Henry faced his first serious challenge in 1487, when the Yorkist pretender Lambert Simnel landed in Ireland and claimed to be Edward Plantagenet, Earl of Warwick, son of Edward IV's brother George, Duke of Clarence, and rightful King of England. Simnel's chief promoters were Edward IV's sister, Margaret of York, dowager Duchess of Burgundy, and her nephew, John de la Pole, Earl of Lincoln. Henry VII had taken the sensible precaution of confining the real Earl of Warwick to the Tower of London at the start of his reign and so now had him brought out of the Tower and paraded through the streets of London. Strangely, this failed to deter Simnel's Yorkist supporters, who crowned him 'King Edward VI' in Dublin Cathedral on 24 May 1487 and continued to make plans to invade England. Simnel and Lincoln's army landed in Lancashire on 5 June 1487 but was defeated eleven days later by the King's superior forces at Stoke-by-Newark in Nottinghamshire. Lincoln was killed alongside hundreds of Irish soldiers and Simnel was captured and pardoned by Henry, who gave him a post in the royal kitchens.

Perkin Warbeck, a native of Tournai in Picardy, posed a far more significant threat to the newly established Tudor dynasty and caused Henry VII considerable trouble for much of the 1490s. It was in Ireland in 1491 that Warbeck first assumed the identity of Richard, Duke of York, second son of Edward IV, who had been murdered in the Tower with his older brother Edward V ten years earlier. For the next four years, Warbeck toured the courts of Europe attempting to gather support from Henry's enemies. He was initially welcomed by Charles VIII of France but then expelled in 1492 under the terms of the Treaty of Étaples, which stipulated that the French would not provide support to any Yorkist rebels against Henry VII. Warbeck then moved to Burgundy, where Margaret of York publicly recognized him as her nephew, styling him 'The White Rose of England'. Henry VII's decision to invest his three-year-old son Prince Henry as Duke of York in November 1494 was a direct response to the pretender.

In 1495, Warbeck sailed from Flanders with a small army, provided again by Margaret of York, and attempted to land at Deal in Kent on 3 July. But Henry was forewarned and Warbeck's men were roundly defeated by the King's forces. Warbeck fled to Scotland, where he found favour with King James IV, who married him to his cousin, Lady Catherine Gordon. It was from the Scottish court in Edinburgh that Warbeck sent this letter to Bernard de la Forsa, Edward IV's former envoy to the Spanish court, boldly signing himself 'Your friend Richard of England'. Warbeck entreats de la Forsa to use his influence with his friends in Spain in order to win the backing of Henry's principal overseas ally, King Ferdinand II of Aragon, to help him recover his 'right in England'. This is one of only two letters by Warbeck to have survived. The other was sent to Queen Isabella I of Castile from 'Your cousin Richard Plantagenet, second son of the late King Edward, Duke of York', and sought Isabella's mediation to win backing from her husband, King Ferdinand. Both Ferdinand and Isabella spurned Warbeck's request for help.

In September 1496, James IV and Warbeck launched a joint invasion of England, but the north held firm under the command of the Earl of Surrey. James IV and Warbeck withdrew but Henry VII decided to launch a counter-invasion and secured consent from Parliament to levy taxation for war. The Cornish, however, refused to contribute to the cost of a war in faraway Scotland and rebelled against Henry's burdensome fiscal demands. The insurgents marched unopposed across southern England towards London but were finally defeated on 17 June 1497 at Blackheath, less than a mile from Greenwich Palace. Warbeck decided to take advantage of the unrest in England and sailed for Cornwall. He landed near Land's End and found support among the aggrieved Cornishmen, who declared him King Richard IV. With a Cornish army of 6,000 men, Warbeck marched towards London, but when his forces crumbled in the face of Henry's army Warbeck lost his nerve and was captured attempting to seek sanctuary in Beaulieu Abbey. Henry VII had the imposter taken to London where he was imprisoned in the Tower, alongside Edward, Earl of Warwick, a genuine Yorkist prince. The two were executed in November 1499.

Ill͞ma atqȝ excell͞ma D͞na Sponsa mea cariss͞ma plurima cū precipua c͞ome
datione Salutē. Legi suauissimas l͞ras u͞re Cel.mⁱˢ nouissime ad me datas. qȝ
Integerrimū u͞rm erga me amorē facile conspexi. Ita nempe me recrearūt
ᵽse l͞re u͞re propria u͞ra manu exscripte Ita qȝ hylare et iucudū reddid.
ut et u͞ra Cel.mᵗ viderer Intueri / et preclariss͞ma mea sponsa affari et a
plecti. Dicere n͞o posse quāto desydexio videndi u͞ra Subl͞teⁱ teneor / q͞n
qȝ sit mihi molesta ista tanta perastinatio u͞ri ad me aduent͞. Habe
qras Immortales u͞re subl͞ti qᵉ huic meo tā ardenti In se amorⁱ, tā amā
corespondeat. Pergat Itaqȝ oro ut cepit / et sicuti ego siu noctos et dies
dulce memoria teneo. Ita quoqȝ et Ipsa meū recens nomie I suo ᵽ pecto
seruet / suūqȝ ad me aduentū maturet. ut ex absentibȝ siūg p͞ntes. et con
ceptus Inter nos amor / ac sperata gaudia suos aliquādo fructⁱ decerpat
Ceterū (quod mihi u͞ra claritas Iniuxit) sū executⁱ In c͞omendanda sc
Illa Sere.mⁱˢ d͞mⁱˢ regi et regine parentibȝ meis / atqȝ In declaranda filiali vi
erga Illos obseruantia. quod quidez fuit Illis pgratū audire (me potiſ
simū referente. Placeat Itaqȝ obsecro u͞re quoqȝ Cel.mⁱ mutuas In hoc
genere officⁱ mihi vices reddere. Et Sere.mⁱˢ D͞mⁱˢ meis u͞ris parentibȝ me
ex Intimo corde c͞omendare. Eos aut n͞o setus q͞m si mei proprⁱ pare
tes eent. sūmopᵉ colo. veneror. et obseruo. atqȝ Illis felicia et ᵽspa cūc
cupio. Restat ut u͞ra Subl͞tas felix et fausta sit. Leta qȝ sese seruet
Incolumē. Suis demⁱqȝ l͞ris crebro et sepe me uisere velit. Quod est futu
rū mihi q͞m iucūdissimū. Ex Castello m͞eo Ludlo iⁱⁱ Nonas octob. Amo. I

De Arturo Principe de Inglaterra
a la Princesta D. Catalina Su esposa

E. D. Cel.mⁱˢ   amantiss͞mⁱ Sponsus E Arthur͞ princep͞
                     Vallie Dux comūbⁱ et Rex͞ⁱⁱⁱs primogen͞

The Spanish Marriage

Autograph letter by Prince Arthur, to Katherine of Aragon, expressing his love for her and his eagerness to meet her. Ludlow Castle, 5 October 1499.

British Library, Egerton MS 616, f. 14

Most illustrious and most excellent lady, my dearest spouse, I wish you very much health, with my hearty commendation.

I have read the most sweet letters of your Highness lately given to me, from which I have easily perceived your most entire love to me. Truly, your letters, traced by your own hand, have so delighted me, and have rendered me so cheerful and jocund, that I fancied I beheld your Highness and conversed with and embraced my dearest wife. I cannot tell you what an earnest desire I feel to see your Highness, and how vexatious to me is this procrastination about your coming. I owe eternal thanks to your excellence that you so lovingly correspond to this my so ardent love. Let it continue, I entreat, as it has begun; and, like I cherish your sweet remembrance night and day, so do you preserve my name ever fresh in your breast. And let your coming to me be hastened, that instead of being absent we may be present with each other, and the love conceived between us and the wished-for joys may reap their proper fruit.

Moreover I have done as your illustrious Highness enjoined me, that is to say, in commending you to the most serene lord and lady King and Queen my parents, and in declaring your filial regard towards them, which to them was most pleasing to hear, especially from my lips. I also beseech your Highness that it may please you to exercise a similar good office for me and to commend me with hearty good will to my most serene lord and lady your parents; for I greatly value, venerate, and esteem them, even as though they were my own, and wish them all happiness and prosperity.

May your Highness be ever fortunate and happy, and be kept safe and joyful, and let me know it often and speedily by your letters, which will be to me most joyous.

Your Highness' loving spouse, Arthur, Prince of Wales, Duke of Cornwall, eldest son of the King.

Throughout his reign, Henry VII pursued a defensive foreign policy designed to neutralize the capacity of France, Spain, Burgundy and Scotland and to eliminate Yorkist pretenders. Henry also shrewdly arranged strategic marriages for his children to bolster the new Tudor dynasty by linking it into a network of European royalty. In March 1488, Henry began talks with Ferdinand II of Aragon and Isabella I of Castile to negotiate an alliance with Spain which would be cemented by the marriage of his eldest son and heir, Prince Arthur, to their youngest daughter, Katherine of Aragon. Ferdinand and Isabella's own marriage in 1469 had united the kingdoms of Aragon and Castile under their joint rule and transformed Spain into a major European power. In 1492, Ferdinand and Isabella conquered the kingdom of Granada, the last stronghold of Moorish Spain and, in the same year, Christopher Columbus voyaged to the continent of America under their patronage, giving Spain a rich and powerful empire in the New World. Ferdinand and Isabella also instituted the Spanish Inquisition and ordered the conversion or expulsion of their Jewish and Moorish subjects, as a consequence of which Pope Alexander VI awarded them the title of *Los Reyes Católicos* (The Catholic Kings) for ardently championing the Catholic faith. Given the power, prestige and wealth of the Spanish monarchs, it is little wonder that Henry VII was keen to marry his heir to their eligible daughter.

On 27 March 1489, the Anglo–Spanish Treaty of Medina del Campo was concluded and Arthur and Katherine, then aged just two and three respectively, were pledged to be married when they came of age. This was an impressive achievement for newcomer Henry and a welcome stamp of international approval for the fledgling Tudor dynasty. Critically, the alliance also meant that Spain was now closed to Yorkist pretenders. Henry's crushing of the Cornish rebellion in 1497 cleared the way for the formal betrothal by proxy of Katherine to Arthur. The ceremony took place on 15 August 1497 at the ancient palace of Woodstock in Oxfordshire, with the Spanish ambassador, Rodrigo Gonzalez de Puebla, standing in for the bride. On this occasion the oaths were taken *per verba de futuro*, thus indicating a promise of future intent. On 19 May 1499, shortly before Katherine was due to travel to England, the young couple were married by proxy at Tickenhill Manor near Ludlow and this time the oaths taken were *per verba de praesenti*, fully committing them from that point on to their marriage. Again, Katherine was represented by Gonzalez de Puebla, who was authorized to conclude an indissoluble marriage in her name.

Katherine's departure from Spain was delayed by disputes between Henry VII and Ferdinand over the payment of her dowry. Katherine's parents were also quite naturally concerned about the insecurity of the Tudor dynasty and refused to let her set out for England until Perkin Warbeck, already imprisoned in the Tower, had been removed so that he could no longer pose a threat to the stability of the realm. Even after Warbeck's execution, however, two more years were to elapse before Arthur would see his bride-to-be. Until then, the couple maintained their courtship by correspondence, always writing in Latin because neither of them understood the other's native tongue. This is one of several letters that Arthur sent to Katherine, his 'dearest spouse'. Writing in a small, neat hand, Arthur thanked her for her sweet letters and confessed an earnest desire to see her: 'let your coming to me be hastened, that instead of being absent we may be present with each other, and the love conceived between us and the wished-for joys may reap their proper fruit'. Katherine and Arthur were only thirteen at the time, but they would have been fully aware that they were expected to ensure the perpetuation of the Tudor dynasty through the birth of a male heir – the 'proper fruit'.

A Spanish Princess

Autograph draft letter, unsigned, by Henry VII, to Katherine of Aragon, conveying his pleasure and anticipation at the news of her arrival in England. Richmond Palace, October 1501.

This letter was badly damaged in the Cotton fire of 1731 but it has been possible to reconstruct portions of the text by using transcriptions made before that date. Recovered words are placed within square brackets and lost portions are indicated by ellipses.

British Library, Cotton MS Galba B ii, f. 154r–v

[Madam, [your late arrival] here in our realm
is to us so … and so very agreeable that we cannot adequately
say or express the great pleasure, joy, [and]
relief which we feel, nor the anticipation of seeing your
noble presence, which we have often desired,
both for the great graces and virtues which we hear
it has pleased [God] to give to your person, and also [for the]
mutual amity, confederation, and good alliance
between our good cousins the King and Queen of Spain [your]
parents and us, which [your presence] will now
greatly augment, and also
our great affection for them.

Madam it has likewise been [very satisfactory]
[to us] that you have avoided and passed the great [dangers and perils]
of the sea, and you and your fair company
have arrived [here in a] port of safety, …
… us, and we give thanks to God for all …
And for the rest, madam, we offer
and give you all the comforts and [advantages]
that are available in our realm, for
the benefit of your good pleasure and will.

...

*[Madam,] I [beseech you that] it may please you to regard us
henceforward as your good and [loving]
father, as familiarly as you would do the King and Queen [your]
parents, for on our part we are resolved and [determined]
to treat, welcome and favour you like our
own daughter, and to treat you in the same manner
as any our own children.*

*Madam, it is not possible for me to [meet] you
on your arrival, nor to receive you as well and favourably [as]
my heart desires, and as your virtues
merit, but at least, madam, may it please you
to be sure of my sincere intentions and to have [patience].*

Madame [...] porza [...]
noz est tant [...] et paisible / q bonne met
stanuous dire ne exprymer le grant plaisr [...]
cosolacion q noz en anous / et espalemet de boir [...]
noble presence / ce q anous sommes efforz desire [...]
tant pñ les grans graces q vertuz q entendons [...]
q sa grace [...] attribuer a vñe personne q auss [...]
mutuelle amytie cofederacion et bonne allian [...]
entre noz bons cousins lez roy q royñe despar [...]
[...] q noz / la qñe a este forz sera par vo [...]
q grandement augmentee / q aussi pñ
[...] affecion q leur portons /   134

Madame semblablemet / ce noz a este [...]
[...] q voyanz enade q passe lez grand [...]
[...] de la mer / et q este[...]raybe a bo [...]
[...] de salut bon et vñe belle copangñi [...]
[...]nous q kepracions dieu d tout [...]
[...] surplus Madame noz vos eff [...]
[...]mmons touz les comodites / ce a [...]
[...] en ya en nñe royaume pñ no [...]
[...]met a vñe bon plaisr q vol [...]
[...]nier

BRITISH
MUSEUM

[...] et Reppntez deroz [...] one vre boy et a

[...] aussi familiere met q̃ forez lez Roy ⁊ Royne

varoud/ car de nr̃e part nous somez Resoluz de [...]

de vous trattez brouillez ⁊ fauorisez come nr̃e [...]

naturelle fille/ et en auecme mamere plub [...]

[...] q̃ mez de noz propres ⁊ naturelz enfans

dame il ne [~~mest~~] est bonne met possible de vous

[...] bonne/ne de boy Recpnon si bien ⁊ fauo [...]

[...] ⁊ contraire le desire/ q̃ voz vertuz ⁊ [...]

[...] mad amiour madame voz plussz

[...] entre ⁊ contraire et de prendre en pa [...]

B y 1500, Henry VII was eager to secure the Spanish prize for which he had long been negotiating. As he grew increasingly impatient he wrote letters to Ferdinand II of Aragon and and Isabella I of Castille, pressing them to set the date for their daughter Katherine's departure for England. The Spanish monarchs assured Henry VII that their daughter would travel to England at the end of the summer that year. Their fears for her safety had no doubt been somewhat assuaged by the executions of Perkin Warbeck and Edward, Earl of Warwick, for on 11 January 1500, the Spanish ambassador Rodrigo Gonzalez de Puebla had informed the Spanish monarchs that:

England has never been so tranquil as at present. There have always been pretenders to the crown of England but now that Perkin Warbeck and the son of the Duke of Clarence have been executed, there does not remain a drop of doubtful royal blood, the only royal blood being the blood of the King, Queen, and above all of the Prince of Wales.

However, fresh wrangles and further haggling over the details of the marriage treaty, as well as Queen Isabella's reluctance to let her last child leave home, meant that Katherine's voyage to England was deferred yet again. She finally bade farewell to her parents on 21 May 1501, leaving the Alhambra palace in Granada accompanied by some fifty servants and with many possessions, including her gowns, jewels and gold and silver plate, as well as more personal items such as her missal, crucifix, books and needlework materials. An arduous, eight-week journey across the scorching high plains of central Spain to La Coruña in the northwest lay ahead of Katherine before she could embark for England. After being delayed in port by violent storms, Katherine and her entourage eventually set sail on 27 September; they survived terrifying weather conditions and dangerously rocky coastlines to eventually land at Plymouth on 2 October.

Shown here is the only surviving letter of Henry VII's that is written entirely in his own hand. It is a corrected draft of the note that the King sent to Katherine soon after she landed in England. Along with many other important documents from the library of the antiquarian and collector Robert Cotton, the letter was scorched in a fire at Ashburnham House in 1731. Fortunately, however, the damage has done nothing to diminish the sense of Henry's pride and excitement as he wrote to Katherine, whose arrival in England was a triumphant endorsement of the legitimacy and authority of the Tudor dynasty. The letter also reveals a more tender side to Henry, as he encourages the fifteen-year-old girl to regard him 'henceforward as your good and [loving] father, so familiarly as you would do the king and queen your parents'. He was, he wrote, 'determined to treat, welcome and favour you like our own daughter, and to treat you in the same manner as any our own children'. Henry had sent carefully selected courtiers to Plymouth to welcome Katherine to the realm of England, but he was so eager to finally meet the Spanish princess that he impetuously summoned Arthur to join him and together they travelled from Richmond Palace to meet her on the road as she journeyed to London. Henry and Arthur encountered the Spanish party at Dogmersfield in Hampshire on 6 November and met Katherine with 'great joy and gladness'.

Katherine entered London on 9 November 1501 to scenes of great fanfare and celebration and, after years of protracted marriage negotiations, she and Arthur were finally married in splendid style on 14 November at Old St Paul's Cathedral. Katherine was escorted up the aisle by the ten-year-old Prince Henry and wore a white satin dress and a mantilla – a traditional Spanish head-covering made of lace – decorated in pearls and precious stones. A few days before Christmas, the newly-weds departed for Ludlow in the Welsh Marches where Arthur, in his capacity as Prince of Wales, presided over his own royal council and was being trained for kingship. It was from here that Arthur wrote to Ferdinand and Isabella to tell them that 'he had never felt so much joy in his life as when he beheld the sweet face of his bride' and that 'no woman in the world could be more agreeable to him'.

My most dere lorde and fader in the most humble wyse that I can
thynke I recommande me vnto your goo beseching you off yo[u]r dayly
blessyng and that it will please you to yeue hartly thankes
to all yo[u]r seruantis the which be yo[u]r comaundment hais gevin
right good attendaunce on me at this tyme and specially to the[se] all
ladies and ientilwomen which hath accompenyd me hyddr and
to giff credence to this good lady the berar her off ffor I haue
shewed her most off my mynd nothan I will wryght at this tyme
S I beseche your grace to be good and gracious lorde to Thomas who
was fotman to the quene my mod whos sowle god haue soule
for he hath byn on off my fotemen hydd[er] at as great diligence
and labur to his great charge of this arme good and this myne
I am not able to recompence him excepyt yf fauer off your grace
S as for news I haue none to sende but that my lordes off S[urrey]
is in great fauor w[ith] the kyng her that he canott so forbe[re] the
company off hym no tyme off the day he and the bischopp off
Murrey ordereth euy thyng as myght as they can to the kyng
plesaur I pray good god it may be for my poor hartis ease in tyme
to com they cannot my chamblayns to them which I
will speke bett for my part than any off them that ben off
this counsell and yff he spoke any thyng for my cause my lo[rd]
off Surrey hath such wordis vnto them that he dar speke no
furder god send me comford to his plesaur and that I and myne
that ben lefft her with me be well entretyd such wayse
they haue taken for my self and myne will not cost me...
that I wryt that I knaw not my self to you
grace for I can no langer thys tyme but wyt
these I would I wer wyt your grace now all
Many thyngis mor will I tell and shew
for thys that I can wryght to your grace y[s]
yf wryten but I pray god I may have it
... for my self excepte no more to your
grace ... tyme but our lord have you in my
... wyt the hand of your
... daughter
                                              Mawgret

The Union of the Rose and the Thistle

Partly scribal and partly autograph letter from Margaret, Queen of Scotland, to her father Henry VII, following her marriage to King James IV of Scotland. Edinburgh?, 1503.

British Library, Cotton MS Vespasian F xiii, f. 134

My most dear lord and father, in the most humble ways that I can think, I recommend me unto your Grace, beseeching you of your daily blessing, and that it will please you to give hearty thanks to all your servants, the which by your commandment have given right good attendance on me at this time. And especially to all these ladies and gentlewomen which hath accompanied me hither, and to give credence to this good lady the bearer hereof, for I have showed her more of my mind than I will write at this time. Sir I beseech your Grace to be good and gracious lord to Thomas, which was footman to the Queen my mother, whose soul God have assoyle [pardon], for he hath been one of my footmen hither with as great diligence and labour to his great charge of his own good and true mind. I am not able to recompense him, except the favour of your Grace. Sir, as for news I have none to send, but that my Lord of Surrey is in great favour with the King here that he cannot forbear the company of him [at] no time of the day. He and the Bishop of Murray ordereth everything as nigh as they can to the king's pleasure. I pray God it may be for my poor heart's ease in time to come. They call not my Chamberlain to them, which I am sure will speak better for my part than any of them that been of that counsel. And if he speak anything for my cause, my Lord of Surrey hath such words unto him that he dare speak no further. God send me comfort to his pleasure, and that I and mine that been left here with me be well entreated such ways as they have taken. **For God's sake, Sir, hold me excused that I write not myself to your Grace, for I have no leisure this time, but with a wish I would I were with your Grace now, and many times more, when I would answer. As for this that I have written to your Grace, it is very true, but I pray God I may find it well for my welfare hereafter. No more to your Grace at this time, but our Lord have you in his keeping.**

Written with the hand of your humble daughter,
Margaret.

Henry VII had been greatly disturbed by James IV's opportunistic support for the pretender Perkin Warbeck and so, in order to secure the safety of England's border with Scotland, he resolved to entice the Scottish king into a dynastic alliance by offering his daughter Margaret in marriage. Accordingly, the two kings signed the Truce of Ayton in 1497, but, as Margaret was only seven years old at the time, the marriage treaty could not finally be agreed until a few years later.

In November 1501, as soon as Prince Arthur and Katherine of Aragon's wedding festivities had been concluded, Henry began negotiations for Margaret's marriage to James IV. It was agreed that Margaret would receive the castles and estates traditionally held by Queens of Scotland, including the Linlithgow Palace, Stirling Castle and the rents from Ettrick Forest. In return, Henry VII was to provide James with 30,000 golden nobles (about £5,000,000 in today's money), to be delivered with Margaret. The marriage treaty and a Treaty of Perpetual Peace – the first concluded with Scotland since 1333 – were signed on 24 January 1502. The proxy marriage took place at Richmond Palace the next day with the Earl of Bothwell standing in for King James.

The proxy marriage was celebrated in London with spectacular entertainments, bonfires and free wine, but the joyful atmosphere was soon to be replaced with one of deep mourning. On 2 April 1502, less than five months after returning to Ludlow Castle in the Welsh borders with his new wife, Prince Arthur succumbed to the 'sweating sickness' and died. Henry and Elizabeth were devastated but comforted one another in their grief with the thought that they might be able to have more children. Their spirits were soon lifted with the news that the Queen was pregnant again, but Elizabeth died on 11 February 1503, nine days after giving birth. The baby girl was christened Katherine (perhaps after Elizabeth's Spanish daughter-in-law), but also died a few days later. Henry was grief-stricken at the loss of his wife, with whom he had enjoyed a very happy and loving marriage, and he never fully recovered from the shock of losing both his eldest son and his wife within a few months of each other.

In early summer 1503, Margaret set out from Richmond Palace with Henry VII and 'a great multitude of lords and other noble persons'. In July, they arrived at Collyweston Palace in Northamptonshire, home of Lady Margaret

Beaufort, Countess of Richmond and mother of Henry VII, and remained there for two weeks of celebrations. As he bid his daughter farewell, King Henry gave Margaret a Book of Hours, which he had inscribed with a request that she pray for him. The prayer book has survived and today forms part of the collections at Chatsworth House in Derbyshire. Margaret's enormous party slowly made its way north with great pomp and displays of magnificence befitting the young Queen of Scots, and, on 3 August 1503, the thirteen-year-old Margaret finally met the thirty-five-year-old James in Dalkeith, just outside Edinburgh. The union of the thistle and the rose, which a century later would put a Scottish king on the English throne, was celebrated five days later in the chapel of the Palace of Holyroodhouse.

This is the first letter Margaret wrote to her father after her arrival in Scotland. In the upper part, which she dictated to a secretary, Margaret begins by expressing her gratitude to those who have escorted her to Scotland. She then reports to her father that Thomas Howard, Earl of Surrey, whom Henry had entrusted with her safety en route to Scotland, is in high favour with James and spending much time with him, but also complains that her chamberlain, Sir Ralph Verney, better placed to speak on her behalf than any other, is being ignored. The last ten lines of the letter were then hastily added by Margaret in her own rather awkward and scruffy hand. She apologizes to Henry for not having had time to write the whole letter herself and tells him that she longs to be with him. Suddenly, we are reading the pitiful words of a thirte-year-old girl who, although now the Queen of Scotland, was missing her father and feeling terribly homesick.

Treshault tresexcellent et trespuissant prince, ie me recommande a vous le plus affectueus
et de boy cueur que faire puis. Pource que le chambellin de ma trescheve [et] tresaimee
compaigne la princesse ma femme soy va puisement pardevers vous pour aucunes matie[res]
que dit avoir affaire, pdela ma supplie et requis vous vouloir escripre en sa faveur, ie
prie trescordiallement. Treshault tresexcellent et trespuissant prince que le vueilliez en
sess affaires avoir pour recommande, et me vouloir de temps en aultre advertir [et] faire
savoir de vre bonne sante et prosperite, laquelle ie desire singulierement [et] de tout mon
cueur estre de longue continuance et bonne duree, comme ie vouldroye la myenne propre
et de ma part quant ie pourray recommer messaigier propice ie suis bien delibere de
vous faire le semble.

En me signiffiant aufmplus sil ya quelque chose pdeca vuquer vous pourroye
faire homme et plaisir, [et] ie mettre payne de vous y complaire de tout mon cueur.
Par le boy aide de nres auquel ie prye vous donner. Treshault tresexcellent et
trespuissant prince, bonne vie [et] longue. Escript au manoir de greneubriche le
xvje jour davril.

Vostre humble cosyn
Henry prynce de galles

Henry, Prince of Wales

Letter, dictated and signed by Prince Henry, to Archduke Philip of Burgundy, expressing his friendship and asking him to write. Greenwich Palace, 9 April 1506.

British Library, Additional MS 21404, f. 9

Most high, most excellent, and mighty Prince,
I commend myself to you in most hearty and affectionate manner that I can do. And because the chamberlain of my most dear and well-beloved consort, the princess my wife, goes presently to you, for certain business which, as he says, concern him there, he has begged me to write to you on his behalf. Right excellent, right high and mighty Prince, very cordially I pray that you will hold him recommended in these his affairs; and that you will apprise me from time to time and let me know of your good health and prosperity which I particularly and with all my heart desire to be of long continuance as I would my own. And for my part, whenever I can find a fitting messenger I am resolved to do the like to you. Moreover, on your intimating to me if there be anything here in which I can do you honour and pleasure, I will take pains to satisfy you in it with all my heart, by the good aid of Our Lord, whom I pray, right high, right excellent and mighty Prince, to give you good and long life. Written at the manor of Greenwich, the 9th day of April.
Your humble cousin,
Henry, Prince of Wales.

The death of Prince Arthur in 1502 transformed the life of his younger brother Henry and would also change the course of history. Overnight, Henry, the spare heir, became Henry, Prince of Wales and heir apparent. Moreover, as he was the King and Queen's only remaining son, the future of the Tudor dynasty now depended upon his survival. Henry VII became increasingly fearful for the succession, especially after the death of Elizabeth in 1503 ended the prospect of further sons. In 1504, therefore, Henry was moved to his father's court, primarily to learn the ways of kingship first hand, but also to place him under the King's close supervision and protection.

In addition to Arthur's position and titles, Henry also 'inherited' his brother's wife. King Ferdinand and Queen Isabella quickly started negotiations for Katherine's marriage to Prince Henry, and Henry VII, keen to secure the Spanish alliance and retain Katherine's dowry, readily agreed. However, the death of Queen Isabella on 26 November 1504 brought the union of the Spanish crowns of Castile and Aragon to an abrupt end. Archduke Philip of Burgundy, son of the Holy Roman Emperor Maximilian I and husband of Ferdinand and Isabella's elder daughter Juana, challenged Ferdinand for control of Castile. With Spain and Burgundy, England's traditional allies against France, now at loggerheads, Henry VII was forced to rethink his foreign policy. The English King decided to engineer an Anglo–Burgundian alliance and, in 1505, financed Philip's voyage to Castile. Henry VII also strongly encouraged Prince Henry to renounce his betrothal to Katherine of Aragon and began secretly negotiating new matrimonial alliances between his son and Philip and Juana's seven-year-old daughter, Eleanor of Castile. Henry's youngest daughter, the Princess Mary, was offered as a suitable match for Philip and Juana's son and heir, Archduke Charles, future King of Spain and Holy Roman Emperor.

In January 1506, Philip and Juana set sail from Flanders for Castile to be crowned King and Queen in their new kingdom, but violent storms forced the couple ashore at Melcombe Regis, near Weymouth, Dorset. Henry VII could hardly believe his luck and dispatched Prince Henry to Winchester to greet his unexpected guests and accompany them to Windsor Castle, where they would be provided with hospitality and lavish entertainments. As a mark of friendship, Henry VII invested Philip as a Knight of the Garter and Philip reciprocated the honour by admitting Prince Henry to the Order of the Golden Fleece. King Henry and Philip also signed the secret Treaty of Windsor, by which Henry recognized Philip as King of Castile and agreed to provide military support against his enemies. In turn, Philip agreed to hand over to Henry VII the last remaining serious Yorkist claimant to the throne: Edmund de la Pole, Earl of Suffolk, who had been in exile in the Low Countries. Edmund was escorted to England the following month and imprisoned in the Tower of London, where he remained until his execution in 1513.

This letter, written on 9 April 1506, just before Juana and Philip departed from England, is the earliest of Prince Henry's to survive. He dictated it to a clerk in French before signing it 'Henry, Prynce de Galles' in his bold hand. Henry explains that he is writing to Philip on behalf of Don Pedro Manrique, Katherine of Aragon's chamberlain, who has business in Spain. Interestingly, he refers to Katherine as 'my most dear and well-beloved consort, the princess my wife' even though he had been instructed to repudiate their betrothal the previous year.

Philip's stay in England had provided the fourteen-year-old Henry with a welcome break from the cloistered and regimented existence imposed on him by his ageing and over-protective father. Henry had found a kindred spirit in Philip, who, like him, was young, handsome and athletic and, unlike his father, a role model that the young prince would wish to emulate. Perhaps Henry VII had observed this himself or perhaps, with his health in decline, he was thinking about his own mortality when, bidding Philip farewell, he urged him to be a good protector and friend to his son.

Clearly not wanting their acquaintance to end, Prince Henry ends his letter by asking Philip to correspond with him and promises to write in return. Soon after reaching Spain, however, Philip became ill with a pulmonary infection and died on 25 September. Writing to the great humanist scholar, Erasmus, Prince Henry revealed how devastated he had been to receive 'the news of the death of the King of Castile my wholly and entirely and best beloved brother', and confided that 'never since the death of my dearest mother, hath there come to me more hateful intelligence'.

fe. manera señor q̃ no estoy en la mayor pe-
rreçunjoxa del mundo de vna para ver tod
los niños q̃ estan aca para me yr por dios
esta das de dias q̃ en londres de njos de o-
ri mi persona no me vngo ni aun para
mi casa porq̃ por vyda de vra alteza q̃ a
e hen dydo vnas manjllas para azer
ropa de aseoyo pelo mjgo q̃ mda va
da defuvda q̃ despues q̃ dalla par-
uno esto yo no doy ropas muchas q̃ esta
me en mjodo las q̃ dalla hize mjg na
mjgo yno las de boado por so supe
anta alteza q̃ no ma de pe mi djas ylo
presto q̃ se pudyr porq̃ cueda mjng
no pude venjr desta manera

asy mjsmo suplyco a vra alteza me aga ta
ta mjd de un vjas me vn frayle de la o
den de san ffrancisco de so se manera q̃
a lestado para confesor porq̃ como antes
tja es scrito estas reys yo no entiendo de
lingua y njlesa ni la se ablas y no se
me han confesar y esto ade ser q̃ njo
esa ma ndaje muy presto porq̃ va vas
cua con mjngi q̃ estar syn confesor
pare me val aora amj q̃ aser yo me se q̃ estado

muerte anna aora a nro señor yntercada
por alg.o nuñez anna no le todo venço y en
esto suplico a u.a al.za esta ue.d a u.a me
presto y al dezir q esta carta lleua me
apresto muy byen aora base a casa no
no de nro con.o le pagar suplico a u.a al
za me aya tanto q.d le mande alla
pagar y le aya por encomendado por
q. d nro tanto cargo del q. qual quier
m.d q u.a al.za le aya le recebyre yo en m.
nalada nro señor la vyda y muy p.a al.za
do de u.a al.za guarde y acreçiente como
yo desseo de santiago a xxy de abryll

The Miserable Widow

Autograph letter by Katherine, dowager Princess of Wales, to her father Ferdinand II of Aragon, complaining about the poverty-stricken conditions in which she is being forced to live. Richmond, 22 April 1506.

British Library, Egerton MS 616, ff. 29–30

… *[I cannot] speak more particularly, because I know not what will become of this letter, or if it will arrive at the hands of your Highness; but when Don Pedro de Ayala shall come, who is now with the King and Queen in the harbour, your Highness shall know all by ciphers. I have written many times to Your Highness, supplicating you to order a remedy for my extreme necessity, of which [letters] I have never had an answer. Now I supplicate Your Highness, for the love of Our Lord, that you consider how I am your daughter, and that after Him (our Saviour) I have no other good nor remedy, except in Your Highness; and how I am in debt in London, and this not for extravagant things, nor yet by relieving my own people, who greatly need it, but only for food; and how the King of England, my lord, will not cause them (the debts) to be satisfied, although I myself spoke to him, and all those of his Council, and that with tears: but he said that he is not obliged to give me anything, and that even the food he gives me is of his good will; because Your Highness has not kept promise with him in the money of my marriage-portion. I told him that I believed that in time to come Your Highness would discharge it. He told me that that was yet to see, and that he did not know it. So that, my Lord, I am in the greatest trouble and anguish in the world. On the one part, seeing all my people that they are ready to ask alms; on the other, the debts which I have in London.*

About my own person, I have nothing for chemises; wherefore, by Your Highness' life, I have now sold some bracelets to get a dress of black velvet, for I was all but naked; for since I departed thence (from Spain) I have had nothing except two new dresses, for till now, those I brought from thence have lasted me; although now I have got nothing but the dresses of brocade. On this account, I supplicate Your Highness to command to remedy this, and that as quickly as may be; for certainly I shall not be able to live in this manner. I likewise supplicate Your Highness to do me so great a favour as to send me a Franciscan Observant friar, who is a man of letters, for a confessor; because as I have written at other times to Your Highness, I do not understand the English language, nor how to speak it:

and I have no confessor. And this should be, if Your Highness will so command it, very quickly; because you truly know the inconvenience of being without a confessor, especially now to me, who, for six months have been near death: but now, thanks to Our Lord, I am somewhat better, although not entirely well. This I supplicate Your Highness once again that it may be as soon as possible. Calderon, who brings this letter, has served me very well. He is now going to be married. I have not wherewith to recompense him. I supplicate Your Highness to do me so great a favour as to command him to be paid there (in Spain) and have him recommended; for I have such care for him that any favour that Your Highness may do him I should receive as most signal.

Our Lord guard the life and most royal estate of Your Highness, and increase it as I desire. From Richmond, the 22nd April.

The humble servant of your Highness, who kisses your hands.

The Princess of Wales.

For as long as she could remember, Katherine of Aragon had known that her destiny was to marry Arthur, Prince of Wales, and one day become Queen of England. The death of Arthur in 1502, just six months into their marriage, left Katherine facing a far less certain future. Arthur's embalmed body was removed from Ludlow Castle and taken to Worcester Cathedral for burial and Katherine, now dowager Princess of Wales, returned to London travelling in a horse-drawn litter covered with black velvet. Once it had been established that Katherine was not carrying Arthur's child, Henry was declared Prince of Wales and negotiations began in earnest for his betrothal to Katherine. A treaty of marriage was concluded at Richmond Palace on 23 June 1503 and, two days later, Prince Henry and Katherine were formally betrothed at the Bishop of Salisbury's palace in Fleet Street. The marriage treaty stipulated that the union of Henry, aged twelve, and Katherine, seventeen, should be solemnized when Henry turned fourteen on 28 June 1505, by which time Katherine's parents were expected to have paid the 100,000 *escudos* still owed for Katherine's dowry from her first marriage. Even though, years later, Katherine would deny that her union with Prince Arthur had been consummated, the treaty also recognized that a papal dispensation was required, because canon law forbade a man to marry his brother's widow and 'Katherine and Arthur's marriage was solemnized according to the rites of the Catholic Church and afterwards consummated'.

Katherine must have felt an enormous sense of relief and thanked God that her troubles had come to an end but, unfortunately, Ferdinand II refused to pay the second instalment of his daughter's marriage dowry. Henry VII would not allow her to marry Prince Henry without it and Katherine became a pawn in the two king's complex political manoeuvrings. They also quarrelled about who should pay for Katherine's upkeep and as a result she spent several miserable and impoverished years living as dowager Princess of Wales in Durham House in the Strand. With only her squabbling servants to keep her company and a frugal allowance on which to live, Katherine's existence was a bleak and lonely one. Matters became much worse in November 1504 when the death of Queen Isabella I of Castille considerably reduced Katherine's status and King Henry decided to search for a more advantageous bride for his only son and heir. Despite the arrival in England of the papal dispensation required for their marriage, Prince Henry renounced his betrothal to Katherine on 27 June 1505, the day before his fourteenth birthday. As part of King Henry's new plan to link the Tudor dynasty to the imperial house of Habsburg, Prince Henry was betrothed to Eleanor of Castile, daughter of Archduke Philip of Burgundy and Juana of Castile. King Henry stopped paying Katherine's meagre monthly allowance altogether and her future looked increasingly uncertain.

This is one of several pitiful letters that Katherine wrote to her father, rebuking him for neglecting her and begging him for money to pay her servants. She wrote in Spanish, and her erratic hand indicates her distress as she pleads with Ferdinand to cover her debts 'not for extravagant things … but only for food'. The King of England, she continues, will not pay for anything, even though she has begged him and his Council with tears in her eyes. Katherine reports that she is 'in the greatest trouble and anguish in the world' and has resorted to selling items from her dower plate because she has no decent clothes to wear. Katherine's description of King Henry's treatment of her contrasts starkly with the welcoming and affectionate letter he sent to her on her arrival in England in 1501.

The death of Philip of Burgundy in September 1506 changed the situation again. Katherine became a desirable bride for Prince Henry once more and, for a time, Henry VII was kinder to her. However, Ferdinand continued to ignore the terms of the original marriage treaty and made no effort to send the overdue remainder of Katherine's dowry, constantly asking for more time instead. Ferdinand's refusal to pay, Henry VII's resulting hostility and the poverty-stricken conditions in which she was forced to live caused Katherine to became increasingly despondent and in March 1509 she wrote despairingly to her father, 'It is impossible for me any longer to endure what I have gone through, and still am suffering, from the unkindness of the King and the manner in which he treats me.' Henry VII's death the following month finally released Katherine from the misery of years of financial hardship and emotional torment at the hands of her calculating and miserly father-in-law.

SVPREMVM CA[...]   FIDEI DEFENSOR.

Holben pinx

KING HENRY. VIII.

HENRY VIII

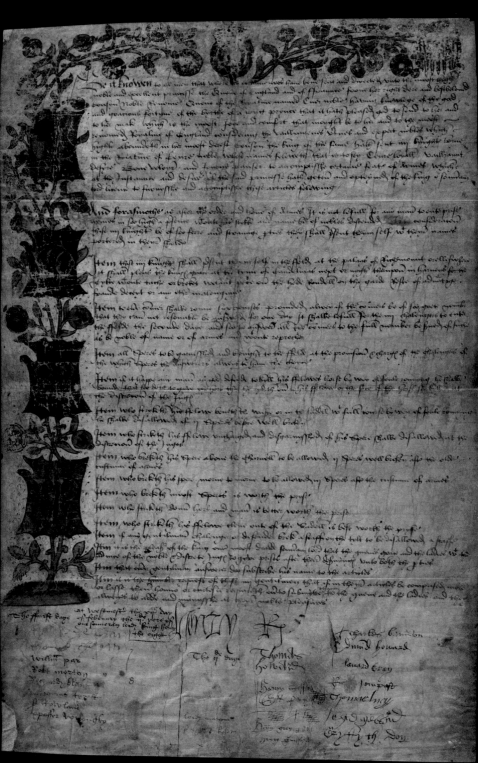

The Birth of a Son and Heir

Westminster Tournament Challenge, issued 12 February 1511 and signed
by those who jousted at the Westminster Tournament, held to celebrate the
birth of Prince Henry.

British Library, Harley Ch. 83.H.1

*Be it known to all men, that whereas certain letters have been sent and directed unto the
most high noble and excellent princess the Queen of England and of France, from her
right dear and best beloved cousin Noble Renown, Queen of the Realm named Ceure
Noble, having knowledge of the good and gracious fortune of the birth of a young prince
that it hath pleased God to send to her and to her make [husband]; which is the most
joy and comfort that mought be to her and to the most renowned Realm of England;
considering the valiantness, virtues, and expert noblesse, which highly aboundeth in her
most dearest cousin the King of the same, hath sent four knights born in the Realm of*
Ceure Noble, *whose names followeth; that is to say,* Ceure Loyall, Valliaunt
Desire, Bone Valoyr, *and* Joyous Panser, *to accomplish certain feats of arms, which
at the instance and desire of the said Princess hath gotten and obtained of the King our
sovereign lord licence to furnish and accomplish these articles following:*

*And forasmuch as, after the order and honour of arms, it is not lawful for any man to
enterprise arms in so high a presence without his stock and name be of nobles descended;
in consideration, these four knights be of so far and strange parties, they shall present
themselves with their names portrayed in their shields.*

*Item, these four knights shall present themselves in the field at the palace of Richmond,
or elsewhere it shall please the king's grace, at the time of Candlemas next or nigh
thereupon, in harness for the tilt, without tache or brochette, volant piece on the head,
rowndell on the guard, rest of advantage, fraud, deceit, or any other malign.*

*Item to every comer shall be run six course, provided always, if the comers be of so
great number that they cannot reasonably be answered for one day, it shall be lawful for the
four challengers to enter the field the second day, and so to answer all the comers to the full
number, be served of such as be noble of name or of arms and without reproach.*

*Item, all spears to be garnished and brought to the field at the provision and charges of
the challengers, of the which spears the answerers always to have the choice.*

Item, if it happen any man, as God defend, to kill his fellow's horse by way of foul running, he shall be bound that so doth to give the horse that he rideth on to his fellow, or the price of the horse so killed at the discretion of the judges.

Item, who striketh his fellow beneath the waist, or in the saddle, with full course, by way of foul running, he shall be disallowed of two spears before well broken.

Item, who striketh his fellow uncharged and disgarnished of his spear, shall be disallowed at the discretion of the judges.

Item, who breaketh his spear above the charnel to be allowed two spears well broken, after the old custom of arms.

Item, who breaketh his spear morne to morne, to be allowed three spears after the custom of arms.

Item, who breaketh most spears is worth the prize.

Item, who striketh down horse and man is better worth the prize.

Item, who striketh his fellow clean out of the saddle, is best worth the prize.

Item, if any gentleman challenger or defender break a staff on the tilt, to be disallowed a staff.

Item, it is the pleasure of the King our most dread Sovereign Lord, that the Queen's grace and the ladies, with the advice of the noble and discreet judges, to give prizes after their deservings unto both the parties.

Item, that every gentleman answerer do subscribe his name to the articles.

Item it is the humble request of these four gentlemen, that if in their articles be comprised more or less than honour or curtsey requireth, ever to submit them to the Queen and the Ladies, and they always to add and (di)minish at their noble pleasures.

The First Day

Richard de Gray
Thomas Cheney
William Parr
Robert Morton
Richard Blunt
Thomas Tyrell
Sir Rowland
Christopher
Willoughby

*At Westminster
the 12th day of
February the
second year of our
Sovereign Lord
King Henry the
eight.*

Henry R.

The Second Day

*Lord Marquis, Sir
Thomas Boleyn*

*Thomas Howard
Henry Stafford,
Earl of Wiltshire
John Gray
Henry Guilford*

*Charles Brandon
Edmund Howard
Leonard Gray
Richard Tempest
Thomas Lucy
John Melton
Griffith Don*

A fter a long and successful reign, Henry VII died at Richmond Palace on 21 April 1509. As king, he had accumulated vast wealth and succeeded in re-establishing royal authority over the English nobility, and on his death he left England at peace. Even more importantly, Henry VII lived long enough to see his son and heir reach adulthood, making him the first king since Henry IV in 1413 to pass his crown to his adult son and achieve a peaceful dynastic succession. Despite all his achievements, however, Henry VII's rule and fiscal oppression had proved extremely unpopular with his subjects. They therefore welcomed the arrival of a new era and considered Henry VIII to be promising king material. He was young, handsome, well educated, musical, a linguist and a great athlete: the very epitome of majesty. Coronation verses composed by Thomas More for presentation to the new king declared 'This day is the end of our slavery, the fount of our liberty, the beginning of joy. Now the people, liberated, run before their King with bright faces.'

Within days of becoming king, Henry announced his intention to marry Katherine of Aragon, claiming that he was fulfilling his father's dying wish. It was a decision that would have the most profound consequences for both Henry and England. On 11 June 1509, Archbishop Warham of Canterbury married the couple in a private ceremony in the Queen's Closet at Greenwich Palace. Two weeks later, on 24 June, the newly-weds were jointly crowned in Westminster Abbey. Katherine was a popular queen and widely admired for her piety, erudition and dignity. Erasmus observed that 'the queen is astonishingly well read, far beyond what would be surprising in a woman, and as admirable for piety as she is for learning'. All the evidence suggests that Henry genuinely loved his new wife; writing to his father-in-law on 26 July 1509, Henry declared 'as for that entire love which we bear to the most serene Queen, our consort – day by day do her inestimable virtues more and more shine forth, flourish and increase'. He assured Ferdinand that 'even if we were still free, it is she, nevertheless, that we would choose for our wife before all other'. Katherine's first pregnancy ended in a miscarriage on 31 January 1510, but on New Year's Day 1511 she gave birth to a son. Prince Henry was christened at Richmond on 5 January and, a week later, Henry went on a pilgrimage of thanksgiving to the shrine of Our Lady at Walsingham in

Norfolk. By providing Henry with a male heir to sustain the Tudor dynasty, Katherine had fulfilled her primary responsibility as Queen. In February, a Burgundian-style jousting tournament was held in her honour at Westminster.

Shown here is the Westminster Tournament's illustrated Challenge, the only manuscript of its kind known to survive in England. Issued on 12 February 1511, the Challenge describes the tournament's over-arching allegorical theme. It begins by introducing four knights or 'challengers' sent by Queen 'Noble Renown' of the kingdom of 'Noble Heart' to joust in England against all 'comers' or respondents in honour of the 'birth of a young prince'. Henry VIII played the star role of 'Ceure Loyall' – Sir Loyal Heart – and wore a costume covered in the gold letters 'K' and 'H'. Leading courtiers Sir Thomas Knyvet, Sir William Courtenay and Sir Edward Neville rode as 'Vailliaunt Desyre', 'Bone Valoyr' and 'Joyous Panser' respectively. The four knights entered the tiltyard on a pageant car decorated as a forest with a golden castle in the centre and pulled by a mechanical lion and antelope. Their shields, which were presented to Katherine on the first day of the tournament, are shown in the left-hand margin of the Challenge, each bearing the initials of the knights' allegorical sobriquets and surrounded by roses and pomegranates to represent Henry and Katherine. The tournament rules, listed in the central portion of the Challenge, were read aloud by heralds before the four challengers and all the respondents – who, in reality, were leading courtiers and Henry's tiltyard companions – signed the document. Henry VIII's large signature can be seen in the centre of the lower portion of the Challenge.

According to contemporary accounts, the tournament was the most lavish of Henry's reign and a great spectacle of Tudor pageantry. Tragically, Prince Henry died just days later and was buried in Westminster Abbey. Katherine was stricken with grief, but Henry seemed less concerned. Both he and his wife were still young and the possibility of another heir did not seem remote. Henry threw himself into preparing for war against France. He could not have known at this stage that Katherine would never provide him with another son.

My most kynd and luffyng brother I recommande
me unto yowr grace as hertely as I can and thanke
yowr grace for yowr kynd letter & for yowr good
councell the whiche I trust to folow for I shall folow me
husband as I am more how luffyngly the kyng my
of yowr duche in me the lord chuttbrlayn to the
whom I besyche yowr grace cum dezly informe yowr grace
great labore & payne the besyche to thanke for the
all ye affort and as talkyng upon a money
I thanke yowr grace for hym of hys demeanes hym
me yowr grace shalbe informe better than I can
wryt as knowthe o lord thn who kep me yowr grace
and from parys the xxday off now ber & by yowr

Mary

Mary Tudor, Queen of France

Autograph letter by Mary, Queen of France, to her brother Henry VIII, written soon after her marriage to the King of France, to thank him for his kind letters and good counsel. Paris, 15 November 1514.

British Library, Cotton MS Vespasian F iii, f.50

My most kind and loving brother, I recommend me unto your grace as heartily as I can, and I thank your grace for your kind letters, and for your good counsel, the which I trust to our Lord God I shall follow every day more and more. How lovingly the king my husband dealeth with me, the lord chamberlain, with other of your ambassadors, can clearly inform your grace, whom I beseech your grace heartily to thank for their great labours and pains that they have taken as here for me; for I trust they have made a substantial and a perfect end. As touching mine almoner, I thank your grace for him. Of his demeanour here your grace shall be informed better than I can write; as knoweth our Lord Jesu, who preserve your grace. Amen. From Paris, the xv day of November, by your loving sister,

Mary.

During the early years of his reign, Henry VIII dedicated himself to hunting and hawking, jousting and archery, feasting, masques and music. Contemporaries marvelled that he could hunt from dawn until dusk without tiring, or dance until dawn with grace and energy. The pleasures of kingship took priority over the business of government and letter-writing, which Henry found 'somewhat tedious and painful' and preferred to leave to his Council and ministers. Instead, Henry VIII was keen to prove himself on the battlefield. For, having been brought up on the myths of King Arthur and the legendary military exploits of Henry V, Henry believed that a king should be a great warrior, and he dreamed of achieving military glory. His immediate objective was to establish his European status and reputation by waging war against France, England's traditional enemy, and winning a glorious victory to emulate that of Henry V at Agincourt.

Henry's opportunity came in 1511, when Pope Julius II and King Louis XII of France went to war over the Italian states ruled by the papacy. Henry joined the Holy League, an alliance formed between the papacy, Spain and Venice against Louis XII in order to drive the French out of Italian lands. To Henry's great disappointment, his early campaigns were a complete failure. However, he finally fulfilled his military ambitions in the summer of 1513, when he personally led an army more than 30,000 strong into northern France. The 'Battle of the Spurs', quickly followed by the capture of both the town of Thérouanne and the wealthy city of Tournai, were the first English successes against the French since the 1440s and made Henry a major player in European politics.

Henry VIII's plans to continue the war against France following his successful 1513 campaign were thwarted when his allies, Ferdinand II of Aragon and the Holy Roman Emperor Maximilian I, deserted him and made a separate peace with France. With insufficient resources to continue fighting alone, and fearing political isolation, Henry entered into peace negotiations with his recent enemy King Louis XII. The two monarchs signed a treaty on 7 August 1514, the terms of which allowed Henry to keep Tournai and entitled him to receive an annual pension from Louis, which Henry regarded as compensation for his ancient right and title to the crown of France. Another condition of the treaty was a dynastic marriage arranged between the ailing fifty-two-year-old French King and Henry's beautiful eighteen-year-old sister Mary, who dutifully agreed to the marriage on the condition that she could choose her next husband herself.

Henry VIII and his court accompanied Mary to Dover, from whence she set sail for Boulogne on 2 October 1514, accompanied by the Duke and Duchess of Norfolk, the Countess of Oxford, her chief attendant, Lady Guildford, and a large entourage of lords, ladies and gentlemen. After a very rough sailing, Mary met Louis XII at Abbeville, where their marriage was celebrated on 9 October. Writing in a hand that is remarkably similar in appearance to those of her siblings, Mary wrote this letter to her brother on 15 November, nine days after her ceremonial entry into Paris as Queen of France. Most members of the party that had escorted her to France were preparing to return to England, and Mary assures Henry that Charles Somerset, Earl of Worcester and Lord Chamberlain, would tell him 'how lovingly the king my husband dealeth with me'. She also promises to follow the 'good counsel' that Henry had offered her 'every day'.

Inconveniently for Henry but no doubt to Mary's great relief, the marriage was short-lived, for Louis died on New Year's Day 1515, considerably weakening the fragile Anglo–French entente. Henry sent his childhood friend, favourite courtier and preferred jousting partner Charles Brandon, Duke of Suffolk, to France to bring Mary back. Before Charles departed, Henry, who understood that his friend and sister had feelings for each other, made him promise not to propose to Mary. Henry was, therefore, furious when he learned that Charles had secretly married the widowed Queen. For a while Charles' life was in jeopardy, but Henry's anger soon subsided and he met the newly-weds at Birling in Kent and pardoned them in return for a portion of his sister's French dower income. Charles and Mary were publicly married in the Church of the Observant Friars at Greenwich on 13 May 1515, in the presence of the King and Queen and before the whole court. Having come perilously close to losing his head, Brandon lived to serve Henry faithfully for three more decades. He and Mary had two children who survived into adulthood, including Frances Brandon, mother of Lady Jane Grey.

Sir my lord hellard hath sent me a lre open to your grace wt
oon of myn by the whiche ye shal see at lenyth the grete victorye
that our lord hath sent your subyett in your absence and for
this cause it is noo nede herin to trouble your grace wt long
wrytyng but to my thinkyng this batell hath bee to your grace
and al your reame the grettest honor that coude bee and more
than ye shuld wyn al the crobin of fraunce thankeid bee god
of it and I am sur your grace forgeteth not to doo this which
shal be cause to sende you many moo suche grete victoryes as
I trust he shal doo / my husband for hastynesses wt Rougecrosse
coude not sende your grace the pece of the kyng of scotts cote
whiche John Glyn nolb brinyeth in this your grace shal see
holb I can kepe my promys sendyng you for your baners a kyng
cote I thought to sende hymself vnto you but our englyshemens
hert wold not suffre it / it shuld haue been better for hym to
haue been in peax thyn to haue this rewarde al that god
sendeth is for the best / my lord of surrey my henry wold fayne
knole your pleasur in the buryeng of the kyng of scotts body
for he hath written to me soo / with the next messanger your
grace pleasur may bee herin knollen and wt this I make an
ende prayng god to sende you home shortly for without this
noo ioye here can bee accomplisshed / and for the same I pray
and nolb goo to our lady at walsyngham that I promised soo
long a goo to see / at woborne the xvj day of septembre
I sende your grace herin a bille founde in a scottyshe mans purse of
suche thyngs as the frenshe kyng sent to the saide kyng of scotts
to make warre agaynst you besechyng yours to sende matherbe helo
assone this me sanger cometh to brynge yours humble wif and
trwe servant
                    Katherine

The Battle of Flodden Field

Autograph letter by Katherine of Aragon, to Henry VIII in France, informing him of the English victory at Flodden and the death of the King of Scotland. Woburn, 16 September 1513.

British Library, Cotton MS Vespasian F iii, f. 33

Sir, my Lord Howard hath sent me a letter open to your grace, within one of mine, by the which ye shall see at length the great victory that Our Lord hath sent your subjects in your absence. And for this cause it is no need herein to trouble your grace with long writing, but to my thinking, this battle hath been to your grace and all your realm the greatest honour that could be, and more than ye should win all the crown of France. Thanked be God of it: and I am sure your Grace forgeteth not to do this, which shall be cause to send you many more such great victories, as I trust He shall do. My husband, for hastiness with Rouge Cross [herald] I could not send your grace the piece of the King of Scots' coat, which John Glyn now bringeth. In this your grace shall see how I can keep my promise, sending you for your banners a king's coat. I thought to send himself unto you, but our Englishmen's hearts would not suffer it. It should have been better for him to have been in peace than to have this reward. All that God sends is for the best. My Lord of Surrey, my Henry, would fayne know your pleasure in the burying of the King of Scots body, for he hath written to me so. With the next messenger your grace's pleasure may be herein known. And with this I make an end, praying God to send you home shortly, for without this no joy here can be accomplished, and for the same I pray and now go to Our Lady at Walsingham, that I promised so long ago to see. At Woburn, the xvi day of September.

I send your grace herein a bill [note] found in a Scottish man's purse, of such things as the French king sent to the said King of Scots to make war against you. Beseeching your [grace] to send Matthew hither [as] soon this messenger cometh to bring me tidings from your grace.

Your humble wife and true servant

Katherine.

Henry VIII's belligerent foreign policy brought an abrupt end to the peace and goodwill that had been established between England and Scotland in 1502 when Henry VII and James IV signed the Treaty of Perpetual Peace. As war approached between England and France, James IV was forced to choose between the relatively new Anglo–Scottish alliance and the 'Auld Alliance' signed with France in 1295, which stated that if either France or Scotland was attacked by England, the other country would invade English territory.

Fearing a Scottish invasion of England while he was away fighting in France, Henry made a final effort to secure James IV's neutrality by sending to Scotland Dr Nicholas West, Dean of Windsor and a diplomat. Following Henry's instructions, West told Queen Margaret that if her husband promised to refrain from siding with France, she could have the gold, silver plate and jewels left to her by her father Henry VII, which had been withheld for four years. On 11 April, Margaret wrote to her brother, diplomatically stating 'we cannot believe that of your mind or by your command we are so strangely dealt with in our father's legacy'. More defiantly, she told Henry: 'Our husband knows it is withheld for his sake, and will recompense us ... we lack nothing; our husband is ever the longer the better to us.'

Henry's heavy-handed attempts to secure a promise from James IV that he would not invade England had failed. In May 1513, Louis XII, King of France, offered the Scottish king incentives of victuals, 50,000 francs and, ultimately, the English crown, if he committed to invading England as soon as Henry set sail for France. Realizing that the Scots would almost certainly exploit his absence from the realm, Henry turned his attention to the security of the kingdom and took the precaution of having Edward IV's nephew, Edmund de la Pole, Earl of Suffolk, executed. The Yorkist pretender and traitor had been imprisoned in the Tower since 1506, but the French upheld the de la Poles' claim to be the rightful heirs to the throne of England and Henry was, therefore, anxious to eliminate potential threats to his kingship.

Before departing for France on 30 June 1513, Henry demonstrated his confidence and trust in Katherine by appointing her Queen Regent, Governor of the Realm and Captain-General of the forces in his absence. To protect the border against a Scottish invasion, he also left the experienced Thomas

Howard, Earl of Surrey, in the north as his lieutenant. Katherine quickly displayed the same fortitude and martial spirit as her mother, Isabella I of Castile, and busied herself overseeing preparations for England's defence by arranging for money, ships, troops, artillery and supplies to be sent north. Writing to Cardinal Thomas Wolsey on 13 August, she told him: 'My heart is very good at it, and I am horribly busy with making standards, banners and badges'.

In late August, James IV invaded England, leading one of the largest Scottish armies ever gathered over the border into Northumberland. On 9 September, the two armies engaged in bloody battle at Flodden Field just south of the River Tweed. Despite outnumbering the English army, the Scots suffered heavy losses and a crushing defeat. Contemporary accounts suggest that some 10,000 Scots were killed, including eleven earls, fifteen lords, two bishops and the Archbishop of St Andrews. James IV also died in battle, leaving Margaret Tudor, now dowager Queen of Scotland, as regent for her infant son, King James V.

Katherine was heading northwards with a large army when she received news of the Scottish defeat. She immediately wrote this letter to Henry at his camp near Tournai to inform him of Surrey's momentous victory at Flodden, which was far more significant than anything Henry had achieved in France. Writing as Henry's 'humble wife and true servant', Katherine jubilantly tells her husband 'this battle hath been to your grace and all your realm the greatest honour that could be, and more than you should win all the crown of France'. She then added, rather ghoulishly, that she had wished to send him the dead body of James IV but that 'our Englishmen's hearts would not suffer it'. Instead, Katherine contented herself with sending Henry the dead king's bloodstained coat to be made into banners. The affectionate tone of the final part of the letter reveals something of Katherine and Henry's loving relationship during the early years of their marriage. Katherine clearly missed Henry and ended by urging him to return home soon for 'without this no joy here can be accomplished'. Meanwhile, Katherine would visit the shrine of Our Lady at Walsingham to give thanks for the victory at Flodden and, no doubt, to pray for a son.

My lord cardinall I recomand vnto yow as
hartely as hart and tonge expres ryght glade to here
of your good helthe whyche I pray þ god may
long contynew / so it is that I have reseyved your
lettres to the whyche by cause they aske long wryt
I have made answard by my secretary to the wch
ther be whyche be so serteyn that they cause me at thys
tyme to wryte to yow my selffe / the won ys that
truste the quene my wyffe be wyth chylde the other ys
that that ys the chefe cause why I am so lothe to
reposy ze to london ward by cause abowght thys tymm
is partly off her dangerus tymes and by cause off that
I wolde remove her as lyttyll as I may now / my l
I wryht thys vnto nott as a ensuryd thyng but
as a thyng wherin I have grette hoppe and
lyklyodes and by cause I do well know that thys
thyng wyll be comfortabyll to yow to vndersto
therfor I do wryht itt vnto yow at thys tymm
no more to yow att thys tymm mitte qd deus
velit inceptum opus bene finiri / wryttyn w
the hand off your lovyng prynce /

HENRY R

Cardinal Wolsey and the Problem of the Succession

Autograph letter by Henry VIII, to Cardinal Thomas Wolsey, confiding in him that Katherine of Aragon is pregnant. Woodstock, June 1518.

British Library, Cotton MS Vespasian F iii, f. 73

My Lord Cardinal, I recommend unto you as heartily as I can, and I am right glad to hear of your good health, which I pray God may long continue. So it is that I have received your letters, to the which (because they ask long writing) I have made answer by my Secretary. Two things there be which be so secret that they cause me at this time to write to you myself; the one is that I trust the Queen my wife be with child; the other is chief cause why I am so loath to repair to London ward, because about this time is partly of her dangerous times and because of that I would remove her as little as I may now. My Lord, I write this unto [you] not as an ensured thing but as a thing wherein I have great hope and likelihood, and because I do well know that this thing will be comfortable to you to understand: therefore I do write it unto you at this time. No more to you at this time, nisi quod Deus velit inceptum opus bene finiri [except that may God wish to finish a work well begun]. Written with the hand of your loving Prince.

Henry R.

Kings Louis XII of France and Ferdinand II of Aragon died just a year apart and their successors, the young and ambitious Francis I and Charles V, burst onto the European stage. In 1519, Emperor Maximilian I also died and Charles V, his grandson, was elected to the title, thus uniting the Habsburg lands and the Holy Roman Empire with the kingdoms of Spain. Overnight, Charles became Europe's most powerful prince. After a decade of pursuing international fame and glory through warfare, Henry was forced by the great power, rivalry and military might of Charles and Francis to change tack and seek to build a new reputation as the leading peacemaker of Europe. His agent was the all-powerful royal minister, brilliant administrator and consummate diplomat Cardinal Thomas Wolsey.

Wolsey had been appointed Henry VIII's almoner in 1509, but rose to prominence when he oversaw the 1513 military campaign against the French and subsequently negotiated the 1514 peace alliance with France. A grateful Henry showered Wolsey with ecclesiastical and secular promotion, appointing him Archbishop of York in 1514 and Lord Chancellor of England in 1515 – the year in which he was also created a Cardinal by Pope Leo X. Wolsey's meteoric rise placed him at the centre of royal decision-making, and by 1515 he effectively governed the realm in Henry's name, prompting the Venetian ambassador, Tomasso Giustiniani, to observe that 'it is essential to speak first of all serious matters to the Cardinal and not the King'.

In 1518, Wolsey responded to the shifting balance of power in Europe by using his diplomatic skill to negotiate in London a Treaty of Universal Peace between England, France and a number of lesser states. The Treaty of London was Wolsey's greatest diplomatic triumph, for it maintained Henry's status as a European leader by transforming him into the 'arbiter of Europe' and earned him wide acclaim. Wolsey's diplomatic efforts culminated in one of history's most famous and spectacular peace conferences in June 1520, when, on the border between France and English-occupied Calais, Henry VIII and Francis I met in person at 'The Field of the Cloth of Gold' at Ardres. Both kings viewed the occasion as an opportunity to impress all those in attendance with their wealth and international standing, hosting three weeks of sumptuous feasts, lavish entertainments and jousting competitions. The ostentatious displays of friendship between the two sovereigns proved, however, to be little more than a meaningless charade. The following year, Henry concluded a treaty with Charles V in which they committed to renew hostilities against France. Two years later, England invaded France as an ally of the Emperor but achieved very little. Humiliated and unable to gain any advantage as Charles's ally, in 1527 Henry once again made peace with Francis I.

By the mid-1520s, Henry's focus was shifting from martial glory to the problem of succession. Katherine had been pregnant at least six times, but only one daughter, Mary (born in 1516), had survived infancy. Though disappointed that Mary was not the male heir he longed for, Henry told the Venetian ambassador that he and Katherine were both young and that, by the grace of God, sons would follow. This secret note sent to Wolsey in June 1518 is one of a very small number of letters that Henry wrote himself in his instantly recognizable, solid and uncompromising hand. It is evident from the note's content that the Cardinal was not only the King's chief minister but had also become his closest and most trusted adviser. Henry confides in him 'I trust the queen my wife be with child' and explains that it was partly due to Katherine's 'dangerous times' that he was reluctant to allow her to travel to London from Woodstock, where they were staying. No doubt remembering past unhappy experiences, Henry adds: 'My Lord I write this unto [you] not as an ensured thing but as a thing wherein I have great hope.' In November 1518, Henry's hopes for a legitimate male heir to ensure the Tudor succession were once again crushed when Katherine gave birth to a stillborn girl.

In cruel contrast, Henry's brief affair with Bessie Blount in 1519 produced a son, Henry Fitzroy, who lived in the household of his godfather Wolsey. In June 1525, Fitzroy was invested with the royal titles Duke of Richmond and Duke of Somerset, denoting his Tudor and Beaufort ancestry; provided with his own royal household, at Sheriff Hutton Castle in Yorkshire; and appointed the King's Lord Lieutenant in the North. Realizing that Henry was considering making Fitzroy his heir, Katherine was distraught. At the Queen's insistence, the nine-year-old Princess Mary, who had been groomed for the throne by her mother, was sent to live at Ludlow Castle to nominally preside over the Council of the Marches and to learn the art of government.

My Lord in my most humble wyse that my hart can [...]
me that I am so bold to trouble you w[i]t[h] my symple
[...] to prosed from her that is mutch desirus to be
I persave be this be[a]r[er] that you do the [...]
as I am most bound to pray for I do know the [...]
you have taken for me bothe day and nyght [...]
my part but allonly in louing you next unto [...]
creatures louing and I do not dought but [...]
shall manefestly declare and afferme my [...]
trust you do thynke the same) my lord I do assure [...]
from you sum neues of the legat for I do hope [...]
shall be nery good and I am sure that you desyr[e]
and more and yff it were possibel as I know yt [...]
in a stedefast hope I make a nend of my letter
of her that is most bounde to be

the wryter off thys letter wolde nott cease tyll the [...]
to sett to my hand desyryng you thowgh it be short to [...]
I ensure you ther is nother off vs but that grett ly desir[e]
mutche more zerouse to here that you have stayd thys plac[e]
the fury therof to be passed specyally w them that [...]
as I trust you do the nott heryng off the legacy wall [...]
vs hw what to muse nott wtstandyng wee trust by your dili[gence]
[w] the assystence off allmyghty god) shortly to be cassd away [...]
no more to yow att thys tyme but that I pray god send you [...]
and prosperyte as the wryters wolde / by your loving
frende

Anne Boleyn

Autograph letter written jointly by Anne Boleyn and Henry VIII, to Cardinal Thomas Wolsey, requesting news about the progress of Cardinal Campeggio's journey to England. August 1528.

This letter was badly damaged in the Cotton fire of 1731 but it has been possible to reconstruct portions of the text by using a transcription made before that date. Recovered words are placed within square brackets.

British Library, Cotton MS Vitellius B xii, f. 4

My lord in my most humblest wise that my heart can think, [I desire you to pardon] me that I am so bold to trouble you with my simple and [rude writing, esteeming] it to proceed from her that is much desirous to know [that your grace does well, as] I perceive by this bearer that you do; the which I [pray God long to continue,] as I am most bound to pray, for I do know the g[reat pains and troubles that] you have taken for me both day and night [is never likely to be recompensed on] my part, but only in loving you next unto the [king's grace above all] creatures living. And I do not doubt but the [daily proofs of my deeds] shall manifestly declare and affirm my writ[ings to be true; and I do] trust you do think the same. My Lord I do assure y[ou I do long to hear] from you some news of the Legate, for I do hope and [pray they] shall be very good, and I am sure that you desire [it as much as I,] and more and it were possible as I know it is not, [and thus remaining] in a steadfast hope I make an end of my letter [written in the hand] of her that is most bound to be.

The writer of this letter would not cease till she had [caused me likewise] to set to my hand, desiring you, though it be short, to t[ake it in good part.] I ensure you there is neither of us but that greatly desire[th to see you, and] much more rejoice to hear, that you have escaped this plague s[o well] the fury thereof to be passed, especially with them that ke[epeth good diet] as I trust you do. The not hearing of the Legate's arrival in [France causeth] us somewhat to muse, notwithstanding we trust by your dilig[ence and vigilancy] (with the assistance of Almighty God) shortly to be eased out [of that trouble]. No more to you at this time, but that I pray God send you [as good health] and prosperity as the writers would. By your loving so[vereign and] friend.

Henr[y R].

Anne Boleyn, the most famous of all Henry VIII's six wives, and the woman for whom the King risked everything, was the daughter of the English diplomat, Sir Thomas Boleyn, and the niece of Thomas Howard, 3rd Duke of Norfolk. In 1514, the thirteen-year-old Anne was sent to France to join the court of Henry's younger sister, Mary, following her marriage to King Louis XII. When the widowed Mary returned to England the following year, Anne remained in France and became lady-in-waiting to Claude, wife of Francis I and Queen of France. The seven years Anne spent at the French court had a defining influence on her and, in 1522, she returned to England as a polished and accomplished young woman to take up a place in Katherine of Aragon's household. Anne was well educated, fluent in French and could sing, dance, play a number of musical instruments and write poetry. The Venetian ambassador later commented that 'Madam Anne is not one of the handsomest women in the world', but her sophistication, intelligence and ready wit were beguiling and attracted many admirers, not least Henry, who some time in 1526 was 'struck with the dart of love'. Henry pursued Anne relentlessly and, even though he hated writing, sent her seventeen passionate love letters, which are now held in the Vatican Library. Even so, Anne steadfastly refused to succumb to the King's advances and become his mistress as her sister Mary had done before her.

Long tormented by Katherine's failure to provide him with a legitimate male heir, Henry began to question the validity of his marriage and decided to seek a papal annulment so that he could marry Anne. On 17 May 1527, Archbishop Warham and Cardinal Wolsey, who, as papal legate, was the Pope's chief representative in England, presided over a secret ecclesiastical court, convened to examine Henry's concerns about his marriage to Katherine. The King based his case on verses from the Bible (Leviticus 18:16 and 20:21), which warned that it was an act of impurity for a man to marry his brother's wife and that the penalty for doing so would be childlessness (interpreted as the lack of a *male* heir by Henry). He argued that, in view of the Levitical prohibition, Pope Julius II had exceeded his authority in issuing the papal dispensation to allow him to marry Katherine, the widow of his elder brother, Arthur. Convinced that his marriage contravened divine law, Henry believed that Katherine's failure to have a son was a clear sign of God's wrath and punishment. Inconveniently for Henry, Katherine insisted that, due to Arthur's poor health, her first marriage had never been consummated and therefore did not contravene the Levitical injunction or invalidate her second marriage.

Henry fully expected Pope Clement VII to come to his aid and quickly resolve his 'great matter' by granting him an annulment. However, on 6 May 1527, Katherine's nephew, Emperor Charles V, had sacked Rome and taken the Pope prisoner, making it impossible for him to accede to Henry's wishes. When news reached England of the sack of Rome, Henry realized that Clement would not defy Charles by annulling his aunt's marriage, and turned to Wolsey, his trusted minister and senior churchman, to find an alternative solution. Wolsey spent the next two years trying to persuade the Pope to allow the final decision on the validity of the King's marriage to be made by judges in England. The Pope eventually agreed to send a papal legate, Cardinal Campeggio, to preside with Wolsey over a legatine court to hear Henry's suit for the annulment of his marriage.

This remarkable letter was jointly written by Anne Boleyn and Henry VIII to Wolsey at the beginning of August 1528 to enquire about the progress of Cardinal Campeggio's journey to England. In the upper half, Anne sent good wishes to the Cardinal and expressed her gratitude for 'the great pains and troubles' he had taken for her. She ended by reminding Wolsey that she longed to receive good news about Cardinal Campeggio. Anne then passed the note to Henry, having persuaded the unenthusiastic letter-writer to add some words of his own: 'The writer of this letter would not cease till she had [caused me likewise] to set to my hand.' Henry, who was by now desperate to marry Anne and perhaps already starting to lose confidence in Wolsey, re-emphasized that the couple were anxious for news of Cardinal Campeggio. Henry was right to be concerned, for the Pope had secretly ordered Campeggio to delay his journey and obstruct proceedings as much as possible. Wolsey was powerless to act on the King's demands.

Myn owne entirely belovyd cromwel I besedie you as yf
loue me and wyl eny thyng to eny thyng for me repare hyth
thys day as sonne as the parlement ys brokyn vp leyng
aparte all thynge for that tyme for I wold not onely
comynycat thynges vnto you wherin for my coffer and
relief I wold haue you gud sad dyscret advyse and oder
but also open the same aduyse thyng thynge regnyng
expedyens to you on my behalf to Go solysytyd ther I for
therfor to hast yo comyng hether assured we out omytty
do to do as ye tender my sower relief and coffert
gyyetnes of mynd and thus shew ye avol sherin dy
m Lett thys Satyrday in the mornyng at the md
and sorowfull hert of yo assuryd louer

T Car hs Ebor

I haue also styyn thynge comyng yourself wych
there ye wolbe glad to her and kndue foyle not sherle
wold her thys nyght ye may returne erly in the mor
agyyn yf nede shuld be vygnyn et erem vale

As agustyn shewys me ster ye had wryttyn onto m
a her wherin ye shuld advyse me of the comyng foyth
the duke of morffleе I assure you ther cum to my han
no such her

The King's 'Great Matter' and the Fall of Wolsey

Autograph letter by Cardinal Thomas Wolsey, to Thomas Cromwell, requesting him to visit urgently to provide 'good, sad, discreet advice and counsel'. Esher, 17 December 1529.

British Library, Cotton MS Vespasian F xiii, f. 147

My own entirely beloved Cromwell, I beseech you, as ye love me and will ever do anything for me, repair hither this day as soon as the Parliament is broken up, leaving apart all things for that time; for I would not only communicate things unto you wherein for my comfort and relief I would have your good, sad, discreet advice and counsel, but also upon the same commit certain things requiring expedition to you, on my behalf to be solicited: this, I pray you therefore, to haste your coming hither as afore, without omitting so to do as ye tender my succour, relief and comfort, and quietness of mind. And thus fare ye well: from Esher, in haste, this Saturday, in the morning, with the rude hand and sorrowful heart of your assured lover.

Thomas, Cardinal, Archbishop of York

I have also certain things concerning yourself which I am sure ye will be glad to hear and know: fail not therefore to be here this night, ye may return early in the morning again if need shall so require. Et iterum vale [So farewell again].

M. Agostini showed me how ye had written unto me a letter wherein ye should advertise me of the coming hither of the Duke of Norfolk: I assure you there came to my hands no such letter.

C ardinal Campeggio finally arrived in England on 29 September 1528, but, much to Henry and Anne's frustration, he ensured that the legatine trial at Blackfriars did not get under way for another seven months. At the opening session, on 31 May 1529, Henry was represented by proxy but Katherine made a surprise appearance to register her appeal to have the case revoked to Rome, stating that she would not get a fair trial in England. Both Henry and Katherine attended the second session; Henry spoke to the court first about his 'scruple of conscience' and presented his case for the annulment, which had been assembled by a team of theologians and canon lawyers working under his personal direction. Then, with all the pride and dignity of a princess of the ancient royal houses of Aragon and Castile, Katherine knelt before Henry and protested that she had been a virgin when she married him and his true, obedient and lawful wife ever since. She then rose, curtseyed and left, ignoring calls for her to return. Letters sent by Henry to his ambassadors in Rome at this time reveal that he still remained confident that the court would find in his favour, but when Katherine's appeal reached Rome on 16 July, it was upheld. A fortnight later, acting on papal orders, Campeggio adjourned the hearing for the summer but, before the court could reconvene, the case was referred back to Rome for the Pope's personal adjudication.

Wolsey had built his career on giving Henry VIII exactly what he wanted. So complete was the King's trust and confidence in his immensely able and dedicated minister, that he and Anne had fully expected the Cardinal to be able to secure the annulment of Henry's first marriage. But, with the collapse of the Blackfriars trial, Wolsey had failed to achieve the King's wishes for the first time and Henry began to lose confidence in him. To complicate matters further, Pope Clement VII and Emperor Charles V had made peace, and in August 1529 the Franco–Imperial Treaty of Cambrai was signed, leaving England completely isolated and without diplomatic leverage. As the last faint chance that the Pope would agree to the annulment disappeared, the increasingly influential pro-Boleyn faction, led by Anne's uncle the Duke of Norfolk, seized the opportunity to challenge the Cardinal's power, which they bitterly resented. Over the summer, they fed Henry with anti-Wolsey propaganda and accused the Cardinal of conspiring to delay the annulment.

The King yielded to pressure and, on 9 October 1529, Wolsey was charged in the Court of King's Bench with breaking the statute of *praemunire* for having infringed royal authority by presiding over the legatine court. In other words, the Cardinal was accused of putting the Pope and the Church before his King.

As a punishment, Wolsey was stripped of the office of Lord Chancellor and deprived of the bishopric of Winchester and the abbacy of St Albans. His assets and most of his properties were confiscated by the crown and he was banished from court to his manor in Esher. It was from there that the once proud and arrogant minister wrote this letter to Thomas Cromwell, his protégé and trusted business agent, who acted as intermediary between his fallen patron and the King. Wolsey's shaky handwriting and his insistence that 'his beloved' Cromwell urgently visit him to provide 'good, sad, discreet advice and counsel' reveal the deep distress and emotional strain he was under following his descent into disgrace. Henry had been reluctant to destroy Wolsey completely and remained in communication with his fallen minister, thus giving him reason to hope that he would eventually be restored to royal favour. It was perhaps to this end that Wolsey informed Cromwell that he needed to 'commit certain things requiring expedition' to him. Cromwell did his best for Wolsey, but he also used the opportunity to promote himself at court and make Henry aware of his abilities. Henry was quick to recognize Cromwell's talent and potential usefulness. By the end of 1530, Cromwell had joined the royal Council and quickly rose to prominence in government business.

Perhaps in recognition of his fifteen years of loyal service, Wolsey was pardoned on 12 February 1530, restored to the archbishopric of York and dispatched north to live out the rest of his days. A year later, however, reports reached the King that Wolsey had been secretly negotiating with both Emperor Charles V and the French king Francis I to obtain a papal order that Anne Boleyn should be dismissed from court. Wolsey was arrested on charges of treason on 4 November but contracted dysentery en route to the Tower of London and died at Leicester Abbey on 29 November 1530.

100. a.

the interlining is all of
king Hen: the viijth hand.

The Othe of the
kinge Hughnes
at every coronation

This is the othe that the king shall [then] swere at
coronacion that he shall kepe and mayntene the right [lawfull]
and the libtes of holy church of old tyme graunted by
the rightuous Cristen kinge of England [to the holy church
of England] and that he
shall kepe all the londes honours and digntees rightfull
[redomines]
and [free] of the corone of England in all man hole
wout any mad of ampyusshement / and the rightes of the
Crowne hurte decayed or lost to his power shall call
agayne into the auncyent astate / And that he shall
endevoze hymselfe to kepe vnite in hys clerdye and tempozelte
the pece of the holie church and of the clergie and
[he shall accordyng to hys ...]
the people is good worke And that he shall
all mynystere
in his iudgementes equytee
shewyng wher is to be shewyd mercy
[and meruge] And that he shall graunte to holde
[approved] [lawfull and nott preiudicia
to hys crowne or imperiall]
lawes and customes of the realme and to hys po

The Royal Supremacy

Henry VIII's Coronation Oath, with insertions and deletions in his own hand to reflect his personal Royal Supremacy following the break with Rome. 1530s.

British Library, Cotton MS Tiberius E viii, f. 89r–v

The Oath of the

King's Highness

at every coronation

The king shall then swear that he shall keep and maintain the lawful right and liberties of old time granted by the righteous Christian kings of England **to the holy church of England not prejudicial to his jurisdiction and dignity royal.** *And that he shall keep all the lands, honours and dignities righteous and freedoms of the Crown of England in all manner whole without any manner of [di]minishment, and the rights of the crown hurt, decayed or lost to his power shall call again into the ancient estate. And that he shall* **endeavour himself to keep unity in his clergy and temporal subjects.** *And that* **he shall according to his conscience in all his judgements minister equity right justice showing where is to be showed mercy.** *And that he shall grant to hold laws and approved customs of the realm and* **lawful and not prejudicial to his crown or Imperial Jurisdiction** *to his power keep them and affirm them which the nobles and people have made and chosen* **with his consent.** *And the evil laws and customs wholly to put out and steadfast and stable peace to the people of his realm keep and cause to be kept to his power* **in that which honour and equity do require.**

Henry VIII ascended the English throne in 1509 as the loyal son of the papacy and Roman Catholic Church. In 1521, his book, *Assertio Septem Sacramentorum adversus Martinum Lutherum*, which denounced the anti-papal doctrines of the German theologian Martin Luther, earned him the title 'Defender of the Faith'. Yet, only a few years later, Henry would turn his back on Rome in order to secure the annulment of his first marriage.

Following the failure of the Blackfriars tribunal and the downfall of Wolsey, Henry adopted a much more radical and aggressive approach in his dealings with Rome. Parliament was summoned for the first time in six years to help him achieve his ends, and, in January 1530, the 'Reformation Parliament' passed a series of anti-clerical laws to attack the English clergy and question the Pope's authority in England. At the same time, Thomas Cranmer, a Cambridge theologian, gave Henry renewed hope when he recommended that universities in England and on the continent should be consulted about the Levitical injunction and the Pope's authority to dispense with it. By the summer of 1530, both Oxford and Cambridge, as well as some European universities, had been 'persuaded' to declare in Henry's favour and pamphlets were published as part of a propaganda campaign to convince Henry's subjects that the Pope held no authority over the English Church.

A team of scholars was also recruited to gather evidence to support Henry's radical claims to jurisdictional independence from Rome and to demonstrate that his case for annulment ought to be determined in England. Monastic libraries were scoured for Biblical commentaries, works of the Church Fathers and other historical manuscript evidence, which were then used to produce a report called the *Collectanea satis copiosa* (the 'sufficiently full collection'). The *Collectanea* argued that England was an empire and Henry, as both its King *and* Emperor, possessed imperial sovereignty, giving him supreme jurisdictional control over both the Church and the State. In other words, Henry's status in his kingdom was second only to God and *not* to the Pope. Readily convinced by the *Collectanea*'s arguments, Henry continued his campaign to 'persuade' his clerics to accept and recognize his imperial authority. In 1532, the power of the English clergy was finally broken when, in a document known as the 'Submission of the Clergy', they surrendered their power to make ecclesiastical laws without royal consent.

By the summer of 1532, Henry VIII was confident that Anne would soon become his wife and they travelled to France to secure Francis I's support for their marriage. Significantly, it was around this time that Anne and Henry consummated their relationship, a full six years after it began. By the end of December, Anne was pregnant and on 25 January 1533 she and Henry were finally married in a secret ceremony in the new Whitehall Palace. The final stage in Henry's long struggle with the papacy was now overseen by Thomas Cromwell, who was rapidly rising in the King's favour. Cromwell supervised the drafting of a crucial series of Acts of Parliament that enabled the break with Rome, beginning in May 1533 with the Act in Restraint of Appeals. It resoundingly declared 'this realm of England is an Empire' and rejected papal authority, thereby preventing the Pope from overturning Henry's rulings on the Church. The Act also enabled Cranmer, recently consecrated as Archbishop of Canterbury, to pronounce Henry's marriage to Katherine null and void and confirm the legality of his second marriage. Critically for Henry, this meant that the child Anne was carrying would be legitimate. On 7 September 1533, Anne gave birth to a daughter – the future Elizabeth I – much to the deep disappointment of both parents, who had confidently expected a son.

In November 1534, the Act of Supremacy formally recognized that 'the king's majesty justly and rightly is and ought to be the Supreme Head of the Church of England'. At some point in the 1530s Henry revised the Coronation Oath, shown here, to reflect his repudiation of papal authority and his assertion of the English supremacy. From now on, instead of swearing to maintain the rights and liberties of the 'holy church', as all English kings had done since 1066, future kings would now swear to maintain those of *the holy church of England*' – but crucially – '*not prejudicial to his jurisdiction and dignity royal*'. It is not known if the revised Oath was ever used, but Henry's added instruction at the top of the page ('The Oath of the King's Highness *at every coronation*') indicates his expectation that it would be sworn by all future kings – including the one he boldly believed that Anne would bear him.

A letter of Sr Thomas
Moores owne hand.

Our lorde blesse you

7

My derely belovyd doughter I dout not but by the reason of ye
counsaylours resortyng hyther in thys tyme (in whych our lorde
for their comforte) these fathers of the charterhous & (as I here) of Syon
iudged to deth for treason whoss matiers & causs I know not / I am
to put yow in trouble & fere of mynde toucheyng me beyng here
specyally for that it ys not unlykely but that yow have herd
was brought also before the counsayl here my self I have thought
yt necessary to advertyse yow of the very trouth / to thynk that ye
neyther conceyve more hope than the matter gyveth lest uppon
other terme yt myght aggreve your hevynes / nor more fere
fere than the matter gyveth of on the tother syde / Wherefore thys
shall understand that on fryday the last day of apryll in the after
as lieutenant cam in here unto me & shewed me that ys
wolde speke to me Whereuppon I shyfted my gowne & went out
the lieutenant into the galery to hym where I met with
some knowen & some unknowen in the way. And in conclusion
commyng in to the chamber where hys mastershyp sat & ye Xtto
as solicitor & mr Bedyll & mr doctour tregonwell: I was offered to
to them whych in no wyse I wolde. Whereuppon mr secretory
unto me that he douted not but that I had by such frendes
hyther had resorted to me sene the new statuts made at the
syttyng of the plyament. Whereunto I answerd ye verely / I
yt for as much as beyng here I have no conversacion with
people: I thought yt lytell nede for me to bestow mych tyme
theron / & therefore I redelyvered the boke shortly / & theffect of the st
I nede marked nor studyed to put in remembraunce / he
asked me whether I had not red the fyrst statute of them of
kyngs beyng hed of the chyrche Whereunto I answerd yet / hys
mastershyp declared unto me that syth yt was now by acte of
plyament ordeyned that hys hyghnes & hys heires be &
ryght have byn & ppetually shuld be supreme hed in
the chyrch of england under cryst / the kyngs pleasure was
of hys counsayle there assembled shuld demaunde
& what my mynde was therein / Whereunto I
good fayth I had well trusted that the kyng
have commaunded thys such question...

The Execution of Sir Thomas More

Autograph letter from Sir Thomas More, to his daughter Margaret Roper,
reporting on his interrogation before members of the King's Council,
on Friday 30 April. Tower of London, 2–3 May 1535.

British Library, Arundel MS 152, ff. 294r–295r

Our Lord bless you

*My dearly beloved daughter, I doubt not but by the reason of the King's councillors
resorting hither in this time, in which (our Lord be their comfort) these fathers of the
Charterhouse and Master Reynolds of Sion be now judged to death for treason (whose
matters and causes I know not) may happen to put you in trouble and fear of mind
concerning me being here prisoner, specially for that it is not unlikely that you have heard
that I was brought also before the council here myself, I have thought it necessary to
advertise you of the very truth, to the end that you should neither conceive more hope than
the matter giveth, lest upon another turn it might aggrieve your heaviness; nor more grief
and fear than the matter giveth on the other side.*

*Wherefore shortly ye shall understand, that on Friday, the last day of April in
the afternoon, Master Lieutenant came in here unto me, and showed me that Master
Secretary would speak with me, whereupon I shifted my gown, and went out with Master
Lieutenant into the gallery to him, where I met many, some known and some unknown,
in the way. And in conclusion, coming into the chamber where his mastership sat with
Master Attorney, Master Solicitor, Master Bedyll, and Master Doctor Tregonwell, I
was offered to sit down with them, which in no wise I would.*

*Whereupon Mr Secretary showed unto me, that he doubted not, but that I had by
such friends as hither had resorted to me, seen the new statutes made at the last sitting of
the Parliament. Whereunto I answered: Yea verily. Howbeit for as much as being here, I
have no conversation with any people, I thought it little need for me to bestow much time
upon them, and therefore I re-delivered the book shortly, and the effect of the statutes I
never marked nor studied to out in remembrance. Then he asked me whether I had not read
the first statute of them, of the King being head of the church? Whereunto I answered,
Yes. Then his mastership declared unto me, that since it was now by Act of Parliament
ordained, that his Highness and his heirs be, and ever of right have been, and perpetually*

considerynge that I ed from the begynnyng well & trewly from tyme
to tyme declared my mynde vnto hys hyghnesse & sens that tyme I
(I sayd) vnto your mastershyp & secretory also both by mouth and
by wrytyng. And now I have in good fayth dyscharged my mynde
of all such matters / & neyther wyll dyspute kynges tytles nor popys
but the kynges trew faythfull subiect I am & wylbe / & dayly I pray
for hym & for all hys / & for you all that ar of hys honorable
counsayle & for all the realme / & otherwyse thay thus I med not
to medell. Whereunto my secretory answerd that he thought thys
myd answere shuld not fast satysfye nor content the kynges hyghnes
but that hys grace wold exact a more full answer. And hys ma
shyp added thereunto that the kynges hyghnes was a prynce not of
rygoure but of mercy & pytye / And thought that he had founde
obstynacy at some tyme in eny of hys subiects: yet when he shuld
fynde them at an other tyme conformable & submyt them selfe / hys
grace wold shew mercy. And that concernyng my selfe hys hygh
nesse wold be glade to se me take such conformable wayse as I
myght be abrode in the worlde agayne among other men as I
have bene before / Whereunto I shortly after the inwarde affection
of my mynde / answerd for a very trouth, that I wold not me
in the worlde agayne to have the worlde gyyyn me. And to the
remenaunt of the mater I answerd in effect as before / shewyng
that I had fully determyned wt my selfe neyther to study norms
wt eny mater of thys worlde / but that my hole study shulde be
vppon the passyon of chryst & myne owne passage owt of thys wo
vppon thys I was comaunded to go forth for a whyle / & after called i
agayne / At whych tyme (as secretory sayd vnto me that though I we
psond & codemned to ppetuall pryson: yet I was not therby dyscharge
myne obedyence & allegeaunce vnto the kynges hyghnesse. And the
demaunded / whyther that I thought that the kynges grace myght
exact of me such thynges as are conteyned in the statutes vppon
payyng as he myght of other men / Whereto I answerd that I w
not say the contrary / Whereto he seyd that lykewyse as the ky
nesse wold be gracyous to them that he founde confor
grace wold folow the course of hys laws towards su
wyth such. And hys mastershyp sayd further th
was na thyng that of oth

now other ways so thycke therein as they be / wherto j answerd
j hym no more occasyon to hold eny poynte one or other / nor
gaue eny more aduyse or counsayle therin one way or other
for conclusyon j cowd no farther tho what so euer payne shold
therof j am quoth j the kynges trew faythfull subiect p
p pray for hys hyghnesse p all hys p all the realme. j do no
harme j say none harme j thynk none harme but wysh
good. And yf thys be not ynough to kepe a man alyue in
j long not to lyue. And j am dyeng alredy p haue syns
here been dyuers tymes in the cas that j thought to dye
one howre / p j thank our lorde j was neuer sory for yt /
sory whan j saw the payne past. And therfore my pore body yt
kynges plesure wolde god my dethe myght do hym good. quod Astell
the secretory sayd. well ye fynde no fawte in that statute / fynde
eny in eny of the other statutes after. Wherto j answerd / p yf
so euer thynke theis seme to me other than good in eny of the
statutes or in that statute eyther / j wold not declare what fawte
fownde nor speke therof. Wherunto fynally hys mastershyp sayd
gentylly that of eny thynge that j had spoken there ther shuld
aduauntage be taken. And whyther he sayd farther that ther
none to be taken j am not well remembryd But he sayd
reporte shulde be made vnto the kynges hyghnes p hys gracyous
knolege. Whereuppon j was delyuered agayne to (a) lieutenant
whych was then called in / p so was j by (a) lieutenant o
agayne into my chamber / p there am j yet in such case as j
neyther better nor worse. That that shall folow lyeth in the hand
whom j besech to put in kynges grace mynde that that
may be to hys grace plesure / p in myne to myne owne
weale of my sowle with lytell rewarde of my body / p you r
p my wyfe p all my chyldren p all our other frendys both
p gostely hertely well to fare / And j pray you p all them
me p take no thought what so euer shall happen me for
trust in the goodnesse of god seme yt neuer so euyll to
yt shall in dede in a nother worlde be for the best

should be, supreme head in earth of the church of England under Christ, the King's pleasure was, that those of his council there assembled, should demand mine opinion, and what my mind was therein.

Whereunto I answered, that in good faith I had well trusted, that the King's Highness would never have commanded any such question to be demanded of me, considering that I ever from the beginning well and truly from time to time declared my mind unto his Highness: and since that time, I said, unto your mastership, Master Secretary also, both by mouth and by writing. And now I have in good faith discharged my mind of all such matters, and neither will dispute kings' titles nor popes': but the King's true, faithful subject I am, and will be, and daily I pray for him, and all his, and for you all who are of his honourable council, and for all the realm. And otherwise than this I never intend to meddle.

Whereunto Mr Secretary answered, that he thought this manner of answer should not satisfy nor content the King's Highness, but that his Grace would exact a more full answer. And his mastership added thereunto, that the King's Highness was a prince not of rigour but of mercy and pity. And though that he had found obstinacy at some time in any of his subjects, yet when he should find them at another time comfortable and submit themselves, his Grace would show mercy; and that concerning myself, his Highness would be glad to see me take such conformable ways, as I might be abroad in the world again among other men, as I have been before.

Whereunto I shortly, after the inward affection of my mind, answered, for a very truth, that I would never meddle in the world again, to have the world given me. And to the remnant of the matter, I answered in effect as before, showing that I had fully determined with myself, neither to study nor meddle with any matter of this world, but that my whole study should be upon the passion of Christ, and mine own passage out of this world.

Upon this I commanded to go forth for a while, and afterward called in again. At which time Master Secretary said unto me, that though I were a prisoner condemned to perpetual prison, yet I was not thereby discharged of mine obedience and allegiance unto the King's Highness. And thereupon demanded me, whither that I thought, that the King's Grace might not exact of me such things as are contained in the statutes, and upon like pains as he might upon other men? Whereunto I answered that I would not say the contrary. Whereunto he said that likewise as the King's Highness would be gracious to them whom he found conformable, so his Grace would follow the course of his laws towards such as he shall find obstinate. And his mastership said further, that my demeanour in that matter was a thing, that of likelihood made other men so stiff therein as they be.

Whereunto I answered, that I gave no man occasion to hold any point, one or other, nor never gave advice or counsel therein, one way or other. And for conclusion, I could no further go, whatsoever pain should come thereof. I am, quoth I, the King's true faithful subject and daily bedesman, and pray for His Highness and all his and all the realm. I do nobody harm, I say none harm, I think none harm, but wish everybody good. And if this be not enough to keep a man alive, in good faith I long not to live. And I am dying already, and have since I came here, been divers times in the case that I thought to die within one hour. And I thank our Lord I was never sorry for it, but rather sorry when I saw the pang past. And therefore, my poor body is at the King's pleasure. Would God my death might do him good.

After this Master Secretary said: Well, you find no fault in that statute; find you any in any of the other statutes after? Whereunto I answered: Sir, whatsoever thing should seem to me other than good, in any of the other statutes or in that statute either, I would not declare what fault I found, nor speak thereof. Whereunto finally his mastership said full gently, that of anything that I had spoken there should none advantage be taken. And whether he said farther that there was none to be taken, I am not well remembered. But he said that report should be made unto the King's Highness, and his gracious pleasure known.

Whereupon I was delivered again to Mr Lieutenant, which was then called in. And so was I by Master Lieutenant brought again into my chamber. And here am I yet in such case as I was, neither better nor worse. That that shall follow, lieth in the hand of God, whom I beseech to put in the King's Grace's mind, that thing which may be to his high pleasure, and in mine, to mind only the weal of my soul, with little regard of my body, and you with all yours, and my wife, and all my children, and all our other friends both bodily and ghostly heartily well to fare. And I pray you and them all pray for me, and take no thought whatsoever shall happen me. For I verily trust in the goodness of God, seem it never so evil to this world, it shall indeed in another world be for the best.

Your [loving father,
Thomas More].

Sir Thomas More, English lawyer, diplomat, statesman and internationally renowned humanist scholar, entered royal service in 1518 and was appointed Lord High Chancellor of the realm in 1529, following the fall of Cardinal Wolsey. More, who first met Henry VIII in 1499 when he accompanied Erasmus, the Dutch humanist scholar, on a visit to Eltham Palace to meet the nine-year-old prince, became a close friend and confidant of the adult king. The two men shared a passion for astronomy and, according to contemporary accounts, enjoyed gazing at the stars together after supper and discussing theology, which was another of their shared interests. As a devout Catholic and loyal servant of the Pope, More used his growing influence in the 1520s to defend Catholic orthodoxy against the Lutheran movement, writing polemics against heresy, banning Protestant books and, as Lord Chancellor, prosecuting heretics.

More had opposed Henry VIII's quest to end his marriage to Katherine of Aragon and marry Anne Boleyn, but he nevertheless accepted the position of Lord Chancellor, trusting Henry's promise to keep him out of such matters. By 1532, however, he was growing increasingly distressed over Henry's repudiation of papal jurisdiction in England and the King's increasing power over the Church. The final straw came on 15 May 1532, when the clergy submitted to Henry's demand that they accept that all ecclesiastical law required royal assent. No longer able to serve the King and obey his own conscience, More resigned as Lord Chancellor the very next day and retired from public life to his family home in Chelsea. To avoid further trouble, More remained silent on the subject of the King's marital problems, but his refusal to attend the coronation of Anne Boleyn in June 1533, followed by the publication of *The Apology of Sir Thomas More*, in which he urged 'good catholic folk' to defend the old faith, incurred the wrath of Henry and Anne.

The moment that More and his family had long feared came on 12 April 1534 in the form of a summons to appear at Lambeth Palace to swear the Oath of Succession, which recognized Henry VIII and Anne Boleyn's children as legitimate successors to the crown and declared Princess Mary to be illegitimate. The next day, More stood before the King's commissioners, including Thomas Cromwell and Archbishop Thomas Cranmer, and declared that, although he was willing to accept Henry's new wife and the succession, he refused to take the Oath, the preamble to which also renounced papal power and affirmed the Royal Supremacy. More was arrested for his act of disloyalty to the King and imprisoned in the Tower of London along with John Fisher, Bishop of Rochester and active supporter of Katherine of Aragon, who had also refused to swear the Oath of Succession.

In November 1534, the Treasons Act made 'malicious' denial of the Royal Supremacy punishable by death. More was interrogated on four different occasions in the Tower but held firm to his principles and steadfastly refused to acknowledge Henry's Supremacy, which would require him to deny his ultimate allegiance to the papacy. Shown here is More's final letter to his daughter, Margaret Roper, in which he provides a dignified account of his interrogation on 30 April 1535 before Thomas Cromwell. More recounts that Cromwell demanded on the King's behalf to know his opinion on the Supremacy, to which More responded that his life was now reserved for 'study upon the passion of Christ' and his own 'passage out of this world' and he therefore refused to 'meddle with any matter of this world'. Then, as if sensing that his words would be preserved for posterity, More defiantly declared on the final page: 'I am, quoth I, the King's true faithful subject and daily bedesman; and pray for his Highness and all his, and all the realm. I do nobody harm, I say none harm, I think none harm, but wish everybody good. And if this be not, enough to keep a man alive, in good faith I long not to live.'

It was not enough for Henry and, on 1 July 1535, More stood trial for treason and was condemned to death for 'maliciously denying the Royal Supremacy'. Five days later, while Henry hunted at Reading, More was beheaded on Tower Hill, proclaiming himself 'the King's good servant but God's first'. Both More and Fisher, who had already been executed on 22 June, were men of international repute and their deaths caused widespread shock and outrage around the world. The fact that Henry was prepared to execute Thomas More, one of his closest and oldest friends, and John Fisher, one of England's finest theologians and a spiritual adviser to his grandmother, Margaret Beaufort, signalled the emergence of an increasingly egotistical, ruthless and tyrannical king.

Remembrance

+ Fyrst for myn expences touching the Busshoppryckes

+ Itm touching the monasteryes of Launceston and other in Cornwall

+ Itm touching the monasterye of Leyceste wch is alredy suppressed

+ Itm touching Nova[m] and others allredy suppressed

+ Itm touching Stanlawe & the Archedeaconry of Richmond

+ Itm for pceding agaynst the Abbott of Redyng glaston and
the other in theyr countreys or ayenst the grey freers or freer

Itm the monasterye of Ryon to be had by pmunire

Itm to Remembre warner for on monasterye

Itm doctor

the lord grey Wylton

Raffe Sadler

Nychas Kustons agaynst grew

Mr Petyngto for on monastery

Mr Longshull for Whalhell

Joh[n] Aromans for Spalding

my self the Latond

+ The plate from Glastonburie w[th] ...

+ The furniture of the house of glaston

+ The Redye money from glaston wth Rede

+ The ryche stufe from glaston

+ The hole yeres Revenue of glaston

+ The dette of glaston a[...] above

The houshold stuf of Dolgyn & Robert Aburyell

Dissolution of the Monasteries

Cromwell's 'Remembrances' or list of matters to be discussed with the King. October 1539.

British Library, Cotton Titus B I, f. 446v

REMEMBRANCES

First, for mine opinion touching the bishoprics.

Item, touching the monasteries of Launceston and others in Cornwall.

Item, touching the monastery of Leicester, which is already suppressed.

Item, touching Newnham and Elstow, already suppressed.

Item, touching Fountains and the archdeaconry of Richmond.

Item, for proceeding against the abbot[s] of Reading, Glastonbury and the other in their countries, viz., Oynon, the Grey Friar and Constantyne.

Item, the monastery of Syon to come by praemunire.

Item, to remember Warner for one monastery.

Item, Doctor Karne.

The Lord Grey [de] Wilton.

Ralph Sadler.

Nicholas Rusticus, Mount Grace.

Master Gostwick for one monastery.

Master Kingsmill for Wharwell.

John Freeman for Spalding.

Myself for Launde.

The plate from Glastonbury, 11,000 oz. and odd, besides gold.

The furniture of the house of Glastonbury.

In ready money from Glastonbury, £1,100 and odd.

The rich copes from Glastonbury.

The whole year's revenue of Glastonbury.

The debts of Glastonbury, £2,000 and above.

The £1,000 delivered to the Lord Admiral.

Whenever Henry VIII came to the throne there were over 800 religious houses in England and Wales. For nearly 500 years, these medieval centres of prayer and scholarship had been integral to the religious life of the nation and helped to shape its society and landscape. As the new owner of all Church land and wealth, Henry was keen to tax it more efficiently, so he instructed Thomas Cromwell, recently appointed Vicegerent in Spirituals and Vicar-General (the King's deputy in spiritual and ecclesiastical matters), to conduct a survey of all Church property in England. Fresh from engineering the annulment of Henry's first marriage and masterminding the break with Rome, Cromwell applied his administrative genius and ruthless efficiency to the dissolution of the monasteries. In 1535, he sent out two sets of royal commissioners, one to assess the finances of all monasteries and churches and the other to inspect the monasteries for corruption and spiritual degeneracy. The *Valor Ecclesiasticus* or 'Church valuation' was the largest survey of property undertaken since the eleventh century, when William the Conqueror commissioned the Domesday Book, making it one of the great administrative achievements of Henry's government. The survey provided Henry and Cromwell with a detailed account of the income of the English Church and revealed the dazzling extent of the realm's monastic wealth. Cromwell's inspectors also reported that the smaller monasteries were 'sunk irredeemably in iniquity', claiming that many were places of immorality, corruption and superstition, while others were falling into decay.

The dissolution process began in 1536, when Parliament passed an Act dissolving all monasteries with an annual income of less than £200 a year. At this point, Henry VIII probably planned to reform the monasteries but not to abolish them completely. The commissioners' report had, after all, praised the larger monasteries as places where 'religion is right well-kept and observed'. However, a serious uprising broke out in Lincolnshire in the winter of 1536 and rapidly spread across most of northern England. The Pilgrimage of Grace, as it became known, was the greatest rebellion faced by any Tudor monarch and was provoked by the religious upheaval of 1536; the rebels demanded the restoration of the monasteries and a return to the old religion. When Henry learned that the great monastic foundations of the North had been complicit in the revolt, six abbots and priors were convicted of treason and executed, and their monasteries were confiscated. Shortly afterwards, Henry and Cromwell began to coerce the heads of all remaining monasteries into surrendering their houses and property to the crown. In May 1539, Parliament passed the second Act of Dissolution, which gave the King title to all monastic properties surrendered since 1536 and those yet to be relinquished. Many more monasteries were suppressed, including Glastonbury Abbey, one of the great Benedictine houses, and Thetford Priory in Norfolk, where generations of the great Howard family were buried. By 1540, some 800 religious houses had been dissolved.

In April 1536, a Court of Augmentations was set up to administer the former monastic lands and revenue. Many, including Anne Boleyn, hoped that their vast wealth would be used for charitable, religious and educational purposes, but Henry sold the former monastic properties and lands to finance his building projects, coastal defences and the wars of the 1540s against France and Scotland. Shown here is one of Cromwell's hastily written 'remembrances' or 'to do' lists, which provides a fascinating insight into the brutal process by which monastic properties and land were appropriated by the King, and then bestowed upon individuals or sold at vastly reduced prices. As the memorandum testifies, most of the beneficiaries were royal administrators, peers and established landowners who were eager to acquire confiscated monastic estates to increase their already sizeable land holdings. Beneficiaries include Cromwell's secretary, Ralph Sadler; his acquaintance and Treasurer of the First Fruits and Tenths, John Gostwick; the receiver of the augmentations in Lincolnshire, John Freeman; and John Kingsmill, Sheriff of Hampshire, who earlier in the year had ensured the election of Cromwell's candidates as Hampshire's representatives in Parliament. Cromwell did not forget to reward himself; he took Laude Abbey in Leicestershire.

Towards the bottom of the page, Cromwell's notes reveal that he also kept a close eye on – and no doubt personally benefited from – confiscated monastic assets. In the case of Glastonbury Abbey, the booty included movable valuables such as gold and silver plate, money, rich vestments and furniture. The abbot of Glastonbury was not overlooked either. Near the top of his list of matters to attend to, Cromwell wrote 'for proceeding against the abbot of … Glastonbury'. Less than a month later, the elderly abbot, Richard Whiting, was executed on Glastonbury Tor.

Right trustie and welbeloued, we grete you well. And whereas it hath pleased the goodnes of almightie god of his infinite mercie and grace to sende vnto vs at this tyme good spede in the deliuerance and bringing forthe of a prince to the great joye reioyce and inward comforte of my lorde vs and of all his good and louing subiectes of this his Realme. ffor the whiche his inestimable benevolence so shewed vnto vs, we haue noo litle cause to gyue highe thankes laude and praysing vnto oure said maker like as we doo moste louely humbly and with all the desire of oure hartes. And inasmuche as we vndoubtedly truste, that this oure good spede is great pleasure comforte and consolacion, we therefore by this oure lettre advertise you the desiring and hartely praying you to gyue to vs vnto almightie god highe thankes glorie laude and praysing, and to praye for the good helth prosperitie and contynuell preservacion the said prince accordingly. yeven vnder oure Signet at my lordes Manor of Grenewich the   day of Septemb. in the   yere of my said lordes Reigne

The Births of Elizabeth I and Edward VI

Official letter sent by Queen Anne Boleyn, to Lord Cobham, her Chamberlain, announcing the birth of a princess, the future Elizabeth I. Greenwich Palace, 7 September 1533.

British Library, Harley MS 283, f. 75

By the Queen

Right trusty and well beloved, we greet you well. And whereas it hath pleased the goodness of Almighty God of His infinite mercy and grace to send unto us at this time good speed in the deliverance and bringing forth of a princes[s] to the great joy, rejoice and inward comfort of my Lord us, and of all his good and loving subjects of this his realm, for the which his inestimable benevolence so showed unto us we have no little cause to give high thanks, laud and praising unto our said Maker, like as we do most lowly, humbly and with all the inward desire of our heart. And inasmuch as we undoubtedly trust, that this our good speed is to your great pleasure, comfort and consolation, we therefore by this our letters advertise you thereof, desiring and heartily praying you to give with us unto Almighty God high thanks glory, laud and praise, and to pray for the good health, prosperity and continual preservation the said princes[s] accordingly. Given under our signet at my Lord's Manor of Greenwich, the vii day of September in the xxv year of my said Lord's reign.

By the Quene

Right trustie and right welbeloued we grete yo well And forasmuche
by thinestimable goodnes and grace of almyghty god we be d[elivered]
broughte in child bed of a prince conceiued in moost Lawfull Mat[rimony]
betwene my lord the Kyng Maiestie and vs Doubting not but tha[t]
for the loue and affection whiche ye beare vnto vs and to the co[m]on
wealth of this Realme the knowledge thereof shuld be wynous an[d]
glad tydinge vnto yow we haue thought good to certifie you of the
same To thentent ye myght not only rendre vnto god condigne thank[es]
and prayse for so grete a benefite but also contynually pray for the
contynuance and preseruacion of the same here in this life to the
god favor and pleasure of my lorde the king and vs and Kinniuersal[l]
wealc quiet and tranquillity of this hole Realme we geven vnder o[ur]
signet at my lordes Manour of Hampto[n]courte the xij d[ay] [of]
Octobre

Letter signed and sealed with Queen Jane Seymour's signet, to Lord Privy Seal (Thomas Cromwell), announcing the birth of Prince Edward VI. Hampton Court, 12 October 1537.

British Library, Cotton MS Nero C x, f. 2

By the Queen

Right trusty and well beloved, we greet you well. And forasmuch as, by the inestimable goodness and grace of Almighty God, we be delivered and brought in child-bed of a prince, conceived in most lawful matrimony between my Lord the King's majesty and us; doubting not, but that for the love and affection which ye bear unto us, and to thy commonwealth of this realm, the knowledge thereof should be joyous, and glad tidings unto you, we have thought good to certify you of the same. To the intent ye might not only render unto God condign thanks and praise for so great a benefit, but also continually pray for the long continuance and preservation of the same here in this life, to the honour of God, joy and pleasure of my Lord the King and us, and the universal weal, quiet and tranquility of this whole realm. Given under our signet at my Lord's manor of Hampton Court, the xii day of October.

In the late 1520s, Henry VIII had pursued Anne Boleyn relentlessly and fought long and hard to make her his wife and queen. Her downfall, just three years after their marriage, was, by contrast, swift and dramatic. Like Katherine of Aragon before her, Anne failed to give Henry his greatest desire, the longed-for Tudor prince. In 1533, the King had been so sure that Anne was going to give him a son that circular letters, like this one, were prepared in advance to announce the birth of the 'prince'. Henry was bitterly disappointed when Anne gave birth to a daughter on 7 September 1533. Before the letters could be dispatched, an 's' had to be added to announce the birth of a 'princes' – the future Elizabeth I. Anne's next two pregnancies ended in miscarriage, the first in 1534 and the second in January 1536. Henry's demons returned; he had expected to be vindicated by God with the birth of a son but now feared that he was being punished, saying: 'I see that God will not give me male children.'

Henry had already tired of Anne's wilfulness and haughty ways and had fallen in love again, this time with Jane Seymour, lady-in-waiting to both Queen Katherine and Queen Anne and the eldest daughter of a country gentleman, Sir John Seymour. The King turned to Thomas Cromwell to help him get rid of his second queen, and Cromwell was determined not to fail as Wolsey had done before him. Together with Anne's uncle, the Duke of Norfolk, he led a royal commission set up to investigate the Queen's character and behaviour. When Anne was accused of committing adultery with four of Henry's courtiers and incest with her brother, George, Viscount Rochford, Henry was only too ready to believe what he was told of his wife's conduct. On 2 May, he ordered Anne's arrest and imprisonment in the Tower of London. Anne was probably guilty of nothing more than foolish flirtation and vehemently denied the charges made against her, but she was famously executed by a French swordsman on 19 May 1536. Her marriage was swiftly declared invalid by Archbishop Thomas Cranmer and the second Act of Succession declared the Princess Elizabeth a bastard and entailed the crown on Jane Seymour's male children.

With unseemly haste, Henry was betrothed to Jane Seymour the day after Anne's execution and they were married on 30 May 1536 in the Queen's private chapel at Whitehall Palace. Unlike Anne Boleyn, Jane was commended for her gentleness, virtue and dignified manner, and John Russell, Earl of Bedford, commented that she had brought the King 'out of hell into heaven'. Jane also strived to reconcile Henry with his eldest daughter Mary, for whom she felt great affection and held fond memories from her time in Queen Katherine's household. Henry had banished Mary from court when she refused to recognize his marriage to Anne Boleyn and further humiliated his daughter by demoting her from Princess to Lady Mary and sending her to Hatfield House to serve as lady-in-waiting to her half-sister, the Princess Elizabeth. Most cruelly, Henry had refused to let Mary visit her mother as she lay dying, probably of cancer, in Kimbolton Castle. With Jane's encouragement, however, Henry agreed to his daughter's rehabilitation, but only after she had submitted to his will by accepting the Royal Supremacy and acknowledging both the 'incestuous and unlawful nature' of her parents' marriage and her own illegitimacy.

By February 1537, Jane was pregnant and, on 12 October 1537, after a long and difficult labour, she succeeded where Katherine of Aragon and Anne Boleyn had failed and presented Henry with his long-awaited male heir. Born on the eve of the Feast of St Edward the Confessor, England's royal saint, the infant was named Edward. This is the pre-prepared letter, sent to Thomas Cromwell, Lord Privy Seal, in which Queen Jane proudly announced that 'by the inestimable goodness and grace of Almighty God, we be delivered and brought in child-bed of a prince, conceived in most lawful matrimony between my Lord the King's majesty and us'. Henry was overjoyed. After nearly thirty years of waiting he at last had a legitimate son and heir and the Tudor succession was assured, proof for Henry that God was looking on him favourably.

The Queen appeared to make a good recovery following the birth of Edward and was able to receive guests at his christening on 15 October. The following day, however, Jane's condition suddenly worsened and, on 24 October, twelve days after the birth of her son, Jane died, probably from puerperal fever and septicaemia, doubtless due to unhygienic obstetric practices. That same day, responding to Francis I's message of congratulations on the birth of Edward, the grief-stricken Henry wrote: 'Divine Providence has mingled my joy with the bitterness of the death of her who brought me this happiness.'

the 4

x 1

and some amonge other, cannot challenge off truethe
but dothe

or Vsurpe the name of Catholique, no

otherwise then the churche off ffraunce,

Spayne, Portingalle, or Englande may

vse the same, for that thei do professe,

of fayth

consent and agree in vnitie wt other

Churches, After whiche speche the

churche of England and eny other

particuler churche ought to be called

and ys in dede a Catholique churche,

in fayth & part off the hole cnt

and yet in professio off vnter of eny Catholique churche,

And herby it may appere that the

Busshop of Rome contrary to goddes

lawes doth challenge supprioritie and preeminence over al
and to make a manazomie yt shuld be so hath and
dothe wrest scripture for that purpose contrary bothe
to the true meanyng off the same and the auntyent docto:
interpretations of the same so that by that challenge he
wolde not do wronge onely to thys churche of england but
to all other churches in claymeng supperioryte to over
any autoryte by godes to hym & etc

The Henrician Church

'A Necessary Doctrine and Erudition for any Christian Man',
otherwise known as the *King's Book*, 1543. Draft in a secretary's hand,
with autograph corrections and additions by Henry VIII.
British Library, Cotton MS Cleo E v, f.34

And therefore the church of Rome, being but a several church, and one among others **doth usurp and** *cannot challenge* **of truth** *the name catholic otherwise then the church of France, Spain, Portugal, or England may use the same, for that they do profess, consent, and agree in unity* **of faith** *with other churches, after which speech the Church of England and every other particular church ought to be called and is indeed a catholic church, and yet in profession of virtue* **in faith is but part of the holy catholic** *church. And hereby, it may appear that the bishop of Rome contrary to God's laws doth challenge superiority* **and** *pre-eminence* **overall, and to make an appearance that it should be so hath and doth wrest Scripture for that purpose contrary both to the true meaning of the same and the ancient doctors' interpretations of the church so that by that challenge he would not do wrong only to this Church of England but also to all other churches in claiming superiority without any authority by God so to him given.**

Henry VIII's break with Rome had been politically motivated but, as the self-appointed Supreme Head of the newly established English Church, the King needed to define its doctrines, beliefs and practices. Henry took his duty seriously. Documents heavily covered in his corrections and imperious annotations demonstrate his attempts during the late 1530s to chart a middle way between the evangelicals (early reformers) led by Thomas Cromwell and Archbishop Thomas Cranmer, and the religious conservatives (orthodox Catholics), who included the Duke of Norfolk and bishops Stephen Gardiner and Cuthbert Tunstall. The evangelicals hoped that Henry would eventually embrace radical reform but, although he rejected papal authority, dissolved the monasteries, made drastic changes to traditional religious practices and introduced an English Bible, Henry remained a Catholic at heart, refusing to accept the religious teachings of Martin Luther on justification by faith alone and remaining firmly committed to the Catholic Mass, which he heard daily.

The first statement of faith for the newly independent English Church was fiercely debated by evangelical and conservative bishops. The traditionalists wanted little or no change, while the more evangelically minded, such as Cranmer, Cromwell and bishops Hugh Latimer and Edward Foxe, championed reform. The Ten Articles, issued in 1536, were an early success for the evangelicals, for they included a watered-down version of the Lutheran understanding of justification by faith, and recognized only three of the seven Catholic Sacraments (Baptism, Eucharist and Penance) on the grounds that the other four were not directly based on Biblical authority. The Articles also criticized prayer for the dead, the veneration of relics and images, and pilgrimage to the shrines of saints. Cromwell's injunctions of 1536 and 1538 went on to target these aspects of traditional popular religion for being superstitious and idolatrous, leading to the closure of most of England's pilgrimage sites, the destruction of shrines and the removal of popular religious imagery from parish churches.

In the summer of 1537, a committee of evangelical bishops and theologians published a much more radical statement of the English Church's doctrines, known as the *Bishops' Book*. Perhaps due to his new-found happiness with Jane Seymour and the impending birth of their first child, Henry did not read the work before its publication. When he finally reviewed the text he was highly critical of its contents, which were too Lutheran, and he refused to endorse it. Henry entered some 250 corrections into his copy of the *Bishop's Book*, many of which demonstrate his concern to ensure that 'good works' and not just faith played a part in salvation. He also attempted to rewrite two of the Ten Commandments and the Lord's Prayer, forcing Cranmer to point out that not even a king could do that!

By 1539, the new Church still lacked an official doctrine, and Henry was growing increasingly disturbed by the 'variable and sundry opinions and judgements' that were being preached in England. He determined that his Church needed a clearly defined set of beliefs to end heresy. In 1539, the Act of Six Articles, properly known as 'An Act for Abolishing Diversity in Opinion' clarified Henry's position on some of the key issues that had been dividing conservatives and radicals, and laid down the doctrines to which Henry's subjects were now required to adhere upon pain of death. The Articles were drafted and forced through Parliament by the King himself and they reaffirmed Catholic doctrine on transubstantiation, clerical celibacy, private Masses and the Sacrament of Penance. The Articles became known as 'the whip with six strings' for they represented a setback for the evangelicals following their early gains. Cranmer and his fellow reformers were dismayed by their rejection of the doctrine of justification by faith alone.

In 1543, a heavily revised and much more conservative version of the *Bishop's Book* was authorized by Henry and published as the *King's Book*. It confirmed the Act of Six Articles, reasserted the doctrine of transubstantiation and rejected justification by faith. It would remain the authoritative statement of doctrine for Henry's Church until the King's death. A heavily corrected draft in the King's hand shows that Henry was closely involved in its production. As an enthusiastic amateur theologian, he always relished the opportunity to add comments and corrections. For that reason, secretaries were instructed to produce spaced drafts for him. In the illustrated passage, Henry has rewritten the book's attack on the papacy, claiming that the Pope, to maintain his authority, 'doth wrest Scripture for that purpose contrary both to the true meaning of the same and the ancient doctors' interpretations'. This, Henry asserts, not only wrongs God's law but also this 'Church of England' and 'all other churches' in Christendom.

1537
13 Aug.
Cantorbu.

248

My veray singuler good Lorde in my mooste hartie wyse I comme
me vnto your Lordeship And Whtre as I vnderstand that yo
Lordeship at my request hath not only exhibited the Bible wch
I sent vnto you to the kynge maiestie, But also hath obteynd
of his grace that the same shalbe alowed by his autoritie to
be bowghte and redd within this realme, yours payne taken in this behalf I gyue My Lorde for the
hartie thanks. assuryng your Lordeship for the reuelatio
of my mynde you haue shewid me more pleasse herin, than
yf you hadd gyuen me a thousand pounde, and I doubt not
But that heerby suche frute of good knowledge shall ensew
that it shall well appere hereafter what high and accep
table frute you haue don vnto Godde and the king, wch
shall knowge redownd to your Honor. that, besyde goddis rewar
you shall opteyn perpetuall memorye for the same within thi
Realme / And as for me, yo may recken me your bounden
for the same,
And I dare be bold to say, so may ye do my Lorde of Norwiche
Thus my Lorde right hartely fare you well / At
fforde the vij day of Auguste /

Yor own bondman euer
T. Cantuarien

The Bible in English

Autograph letter from Archbishop Thomas Cranmer, to Thomas
Cromwell, thanking him for using his influence with the King to license
the English Bible for general sale. Ford Place, Kent, 13 August [1537].

British Library, Cotton Cleo E v, f.348

My very singular good Lord, in my most hearty wise, I commend me unto your lordship.
And whereas I understand that your lordship, at my request, hath not only exhibited the
Bible which I sent unto you, to the King's Majesty, but also hath obtained of his Grace,
that the same shall be allowed by his authority to be bought and read within this realm;
my lord, for this your pain, taken in this behalf, I give unto you my most hearty thanks,
assuring your lordship for the contentation [satisfaction] of my mind you have showed
me more pleasure herein, than if you had given me a thousand pound; and I doubt not but
that hereby fruit of good knowledge shall ensue, that it shall well appear hereafter, what
high and acceptable service you have done unto God and the King. Which shall so much
redound to your honour, that besides God's reward, you shall obtain perpetual memory for
the same within this realm. And as for me, you may reckon me your bondman for the same.
And I dare be bold to say, so may ye do my Lord of Worcester. Thus, my Lord, right
heartily fare you well. At Ford, the xiii day of August.

Your own bondman ever,
Thomas, Archbishop of Canterbury.

The high point of evangelical influence in the Henrician Church was the publication, under royal patronage, of an English translation of the Bible. In 1534, Convocation (the representative body of the Church of England) had petitioned Henry to arrange for the publication and dissemination of a vernacular Bible. In 1536, royal injunctions on religious matters issued by Thomas Cromwell ordered every parish priest to buy a copy of an English Bible for public use, even though there was, as yet, no officially authorized text. William Tyndale's New Testament in English was the best translation available, but it was inconceivable that Henry, who, in the late 1520s, had actively suppressed Tyndale's translation, would now endorse the work of a Lutheran, and even less likely after 1536 when Tyndale was burned at the stake for heresy. The first complete translation of the Bible into English had been printed on the continent and was the work of Tyndale's associate, Miles Coverdale. It was less scholarly than Tyndale's translation but was nonetheless recommended to Henry by his advisers on the basis that it was untainted by heresy.

In 1537, another of Tyndale's collaborators, John Rogers, produced an edition of the English Bible under the pseudonym Thomas Matthew. Making the Bible available to people in English was fundamental to everything the evangelicals hoped to achieve and so Archbishop Thomas Cranmer was understandably delighted when Cromwell used his influence with the King to license the 'Matthew Bible' for general sale. Cranmer wrote this extraordinary letter to Cromwell, expressing his 'most hearty thanks' and 'assuring your lordship for the contentation [satisfaction] of my mind you have showed me more pleasure herein, than if you had given me a thousand pound'.

Cromwell's injunctions of September 1538 ordered the setting up in every parish church in England of 'one book of the whole Bible of the largest volume in English' in a place where parishioners might 'most commodiously resort to the same and read it'. The injunctions also exhorted that:

> *Ye shall discourage no man privily [privately] or apertly [openly] from the reading or hearing of the said Bible, but shall expressly provoke, stir, and exhort every person to read the same, as that which is the very lively word of God, that every Christian man is bound to embrace, believe and follow if he look to be saved.*

There were, however, insufficient numbers of the 'Matthew Bible' to supply all England's parishes with a copy, and there was also the very real risk that its provenance would be discovered. The problem was resolved in 1539 with the printing of the 'Great Bible', so called because of its size, which was financed by Cromwell and edited by Coverdale. Owing to the lack of printing facilities in London, a licence was obtained from Francis I for the Great Bible to be produced in France. However, the French Inquisitor-General ordered the printing premises to be raided, forcing Coverdale and the printer, Richard Grafton, to flee with the type and printing press back to England to complete the work.

The Great Bible was completed and issued in London in April 1539, and by 1541 more than 9,000 copies had been printed. The Bible's finely engraved title page is thought to have been designed by Hans Holbein and was clearly intended to communicate the message of the Royal Supremacy. It shows the enthroned King Henry receiving the Word directly from God and passing Bibles to Archbishop Cranmer and Cromwell, who, in turn, distribute them to grateful members of the clergy and parishioners respectively.

Henry's attitude to the English Bible was positive and, in 1541, he threatened to fine parishes if they did not purchase copies. It was not long, however, before he realized that making the 'word of God' available to people in their own language had unexpected consequences. He had hoped that his subjects would read Scripture 'with meekness' and 'not to maintain erroneous opinions and preach', so he was particularly alarmed by reports that the Bible was being discussed and debated in alehouses, taverns and other public places, and being read aloud in churches to disrupt public worship. In 1543, the Act for the Advancement of True Religion restricted access to the Bible, and reading Scripture in public was limited to licensed clergy. The nobility and gentry were permitted to read the Bible to their families at home and merchants, noblewomen and gentlewomen were allowed to read it privately to themselves. The Act forbade servants, dependents or indeed anyone below the rank of yeoman from reading the Bible at all. The placement of restrictions on the readership of the Bible in English was a huge blow for evangelicals.

Syr this is all that I have done in this mater and that I have offend
yor magestie theirin prostrat at yor magestie I most lowlye aske
mercye and pardon / of yor highnes. Syr ther was also layde vnto
my charge at myn examinacyon that I shalle dd saynyd
contraryed to yor lawes. To what composytyon may be made by
retaynowrs I know not but this will I saye that I retaynyd
any man but suche onlye as were my howsholde servantes but
agaynst the will god confownd me. But most gracyous soueraigne
I have bene so indon and Sowyd to by them that sayd that
were my frende that contraynyd theirto I retaynyd theyr
chyldren and frende not as retaynurs for theyr fathers
parentes dyd promyst me to fynde them and so toke I them
not as retaynowrs to my gret charge and for myn oby
as god best knowythe interpret to the contrye who well most hit
besechyng yor magestye of pardon. yf I have offendyd theirin thus
knowlege myself to have bene a most myserable and wretchy
synner and that I have toward god and yor highnes behavyd my
self as I owyght and sholde have done / for the whiche myn offence
to god nyghtle shyrn I shall contynuallye kall for his mercye and
myn offence to yor grace whiche god knowyth wer neuer malycyous
willfull / and that I neuer thought treson to your highnes yor
realme or postcryte so god helpe me eyther in word
ordede neuerles prostrat at yor magestie in what thyngs
I have offendyd I appell to your highnes for yor grace
in suche wyse as shalbe yor plesure besechyng the allmyghtye maker
and redemer of this worlde to send yor magestie contynuall long
helthe welthe and prosperyte as neuers yeres to reygne and your
dere son the prynces grace to after days & contenue long as
you and they that wolde contrarye that lyffe shame confu
noryshe at the makyng here. And most sorowffull hert of your
sorowffull subiect and most humble this satyrday at your

London

Anne of Cleves and the Fall of Cromwell

Autograph letter from Thomas Cromwell, to Henry VIII, following Cromwell's arrest for high treason, protesting his innocence of any such charges. Tower of London, 12 June 1540.

British Library, Cotton MS Titus B I, f. 274v

Most gracious King and most merciful sovereign, your most humble, most obeisant [obedient], most bounden subject, and most lamentable servant and prisoner, prostrate at the feet of your most excellent Majesty, have heard your pleasure by the mouth of your comptroller, which was that I should write to your most excellent Highness such things as I thought meet to be written concerning my most miserable state and condition. For the which your most abundant goodness, benignity and licence, the immortal God, Three and One, reward your Majesty. And now, most gracious Prince, to the matter. First, where I have been accused to your Majesty of treason, to that I say, I never in all my life thought willingly to do that thing that might or should displease your Majesty, and much less to do or say that thing which of itself is so high and abominable offence, as God knoweth, who, I doubt not, shall reveal the truth to your Highness. Mine accusers your grace knoweth, God forgive them. For as I ever have had love to your honour, person, life, prosperity, health, wealth, joy and comfort, and also your most dear and most entirely beloved son, the Prince his Grace, and your proceedings, God so help me in this mine adversity, and confound me, if ever I thought the contrary. What labours, pains, and travails I have taken, according to my most bounden duty, God also knoweth. For if it were in my power, as it is God's, to make your Majesty to live ever young and prosperous, God knoweth, I would; if it had been, or were in my power to make you so rich as ye might enrich all men, God help me, as I would do it; if it had been or were in my power to make your Majesty so puissant, as all the world should be compelled to obey you, Christ he knoweth I would; for so am I of all other most bound; for your Majesty hath been the most bountiful prince to me that ever was king to his subject: yea, and more like a dear father, your Majesty not offended, than a master. Such hath been your most grave and godly counsels towards me at sundry times. In that I have offended I ask your mercy. Should I now for such exceeding goodness, benignity, liberality and bounty be your traitor, nay then the greatest pains were too little for me. Should any faction or any affection to any point make me a traitor to your Majesty, then all the devils in hell confound me, and the vengeance of God light upon me, if I should once have thought it. Most gracious sovereign Lord, to my remembrance, I never spoke with the Chancellor of the Augmentations and Throckmorton together at one time. But if I did, I am sure, I spoke never of any such matter; and your Grace knoweth what manner of man Throckmorton hath ever been ever towards your Grace and your proceedings; and what Master Chancellor hath been towards me, God and he best knoweth. What I have been towards him your Majesty right well knoweth. I would to Christ I had obeyed your often most gracious, grave counsels and advertisements, then it had not been with me as now it is. Yet our Lord, if it be his will, can do with me as he did with Susan, who was falsely accused. Unto the which God, I have alone committed my soul, my body and goods at your Majesty's pleasure, in whose mercy and piety I do wholly repose me; for other hope than in God and your Majesty, I have not. Sir as to your commonwealth, I have, after my wit, power and knowledge, travailed therein, having had no respect to persons (your Majesty only except, and my duty to the same), but that I have done any injustice or wrong wilfully, I trust God shall bear me witness, and the world not able justly to accuse me. And yet I have not done my duty in all things as I was bound, wherefore I ask mercy. If I have heard of any combinations, conventicles, or such as were offenders of your laws I have, though not as I should have done, for the most part revealed them, and also caused them to be punished; not of malice, as God shall judge me. Nevertheless, Sir, I have meddled in so many matters under your Highness, that I am not able to answer them all. But one thing I am well assured of, that wittingly and willingly I have not had will to offend your Highness. But hard it is for me, or any other meddling as I have done, to live under your Grace and your laws, but we must daily offend: and where I have offended, I most humbly ask mercy and pardon at your gracious will and pleasure. Amongst other things, most gracious sovereign, master comptroller showed me that your Grace showed him that within these xiiii days ye committed a matter of great secrecy, which I did reveal contrary to your expectation. Sir, I do remember well the matter, which I never revealed to any creature; but this I did, Sir, after your Grace had opened the matter first to me in your chamber and declared your lamentable fate, declaring the things which your Highness misliked in the Queen; at which time I showed your Grace that she often desired to speak with me, but I durst not and ye said why should I not, alleging that I might do much good in going to her and to be plain with her in declaring my mind. I thereupon lacking opportunity, not being a little grieved, spoke privily with her lord chamberlain, for the which I ask your Grace mercy, desiring him, not naming your Grace to him, to find some mean that the Queen might be induced to order your Grace pleasantly in her behaviour towards you, thinking thereby for to have had some faults amended to your Majesty's comfort. And after that, by general words, the said Lord Chamberlain and other of the Queen's council being with me in my chamber at Westminster, for licence for the departure of the strange maidens, I then required them to counsel their mistress to use all pleasantness to your Highness, the which things undoubtedly were both spoken before your Majesty committed the secret matter unto me, only of purpose that she might have been induced to such pleasant and honourable fashions as might have been to your Grace's comfort; which above all things, as God knoweth, I did most covet and desire. But that I opened my mouth to any creature after your Majesty committed the secrecy thereof to me, other then only to my Lord Admiral, which I did by your Grace's commandment, which was upon Sunday last in the morning, whom I then found as willing and glad to seek remedy for your comfort and consolation, and saw by him that he did as much lament your Highness' fate as ever did man, and was wonderfully grieved to see your Highness so troubled, wishing greatly your comfort, for the attaining whereof, he said your honour salved, he would spend the best blood in his belly, and if I would not do the like, yea and willingly die for your comfort, I would I were in hell; and I would I should receive a thousand deaths. Sir, this is all that I have done in that matter and if I have offended your Majesty therein, prostrate at your Majesty's feet, I most lowly ask mercy and pardon of your Highness. Sir, there was also laid unto my charge at mine examination that I had retained contrary to your laws. Sir, what exposition may be made upon retainers, I know not, but this will I say, if ever I retained any man, but such only as were my household servants, but against my will, God confound me. But most gracious sovereign I have been so called on and sued to by them that said they were my friends, that constrained thereunto I reserved their children and friends, not as retainers, for their fathers and parents did promise to find them, and so took I them, not as retainers, to my great charge, and for none evil, as God best knoweth, interpret to the contrary who will, most humbly beseeching your Majesty of pardon if I have offended therein. Sir I do acknowledge myself to have been a most miserable and wretched sinner, and that I have not towards God and your Highness behaved myself as I ought and should have done, for the which mine offences to God, while I live, I shall continually call for his mercy; and for mine offence to your Grace, which God knoweth were never malicious nor wilful, and that I never thought treason to your Highness, your realm or posterity, so God help me, either in word or deed.

Nevertheless, prostrate at your Majesty's [feet] in what things so ever I have offended. I appeal to your Highness for mercy, grace and pardon, in such wise as shall be your pleasure, beseeching the Almighty Maker and Redeemer of this world, to send your Majesty continual and long health, wealth and prosperity, with Nestor's years to reign; and your most dear son the Prince's Grace to prosper, reign and continue long after you; and they that would contrary, short life, shame and confusion. Writing with the quaking hand and most sorrowful heart of your most sorrowful subject and most humble servant and prisoner, this Saturday at your [Tower] of London.

Thomas Cromwell

T he birth of Prince Edward in 1537 finally provided Henry VIII with the legitimate male heir he yearned for, but bitter experience had taught him that he could not afford to rest easy. He was the only one of his mother's three sons to survive adulthood. Henry's own first legitimate son by Katherine of Aragon had died in 1513 and his illegitimate son, Henry Fitzroy, died in 1536, aged seventeen. A second son was, therefore, highly desirable and so, after a prolonged period of mourning for Jane Seymour, the search began for Henry's fourth wife. Francis I and Emperor Charles V's profession of friendship and signing of the Treaty of Toledo in June 1538 left schismatic England in dangerous diplomatic isolation. Henry was therefore encouraged by Thomas Cromwell to seek a marriage alliance to strengthen his position against France and Spain and to counter the threat of a joint invasion. A marriage was arranged with Anne of Cleves, daughter of John III Duke of Cleves, who – like Henry – was committed to Erasmian reform of his Church and was allied to the German Lutheran princes through his son-in-law, the Duke of Saxony. The King's painter, Hans Holbein, was sent out to Cleves at the end of July 1539 to paint Anne's portrait and, on the basis of his 'likeness' of her, a marriage treaty was signed on 4 October 1539.

Anne departed for England in November 1539 and arrived at Rochester Castle, where she was due to spend the New Year holiday before continuing her journey to Blackheath to meet the King. Henry was, however, desperate to meet his bride-to-be and in order to 'nourish love', decided to pay her a surprise visit on New Year's Day. Unfortunately, the King took an instant dislike to Anne. He was almost twice Anne's age, in poor health and bore little resemblance to the handsome prince of 1509, but somewhat ironically informed Cromwell that he found Anne physically repulsive. Unable to find a pretext to break off the wedding, Henry reluctantly married Anne on 6 January 1540. The wedding night was a disaster, Henry reported that he left Anne 'as good a maid' as he found her. By March it was clear that the alliance with Cleves was expendable, as fears of a Franco-Imperial invasion dissipated. Anne was initially distraught when she learned that Henry wanted to end their short-lived marriage, but wisely agreed to an annulment. In return she received a generous settlement and a number of properties, and exchanged her title of Queen for that of the 'King's Sister'. Anne would live the longest of all Henry's wives, outliving the King himself. She witnessed the accession of Henry's son Edward VI and his death, the attempted usurpation of the throne by Lady Jane Grey and, finally, the accession of Mary I. Anne remained on good terms with Henry's children, to whom she had been a kind stepmother. On her death in 1557, Anne left her jewels to Mary and Elizabeth and was buried with full royal honours near the high altar in Westminster Abbey.

In stark contrast, the full force of Henry VIII's wrath fell upon Cromwell, the architect of the Cleves alliance. On 10 June 1540, after serving the King faithfully for a decade, Cromwell was arrested for high treason and heresy and imprisoned in the Tower of London. Shown here is the letter Cromwell wrote to Henry two days after his arrest to plead his innocence of all charges. Cromwell implored: 'For mine offence to your Grace which God knoweth were never malicious nor wilful, and that I never thought treason to your Highness, your Realm or posterity, so God help me, either in word or deed. Nevertheless prostrate, at your Majesty's [feet] in what things so ever I have offended I appeal to your Highness for mercy, grace and pardon.' Cromwell's pleas were ignored and his conservative enemies, led by the Duke of Norfolk and Stephen Gardiner, Bishop of Winchester, who deeply resented his influence over the King, seized the opportunity to further poison the King's mind against him. On 29 June, Parliament sentenced Cromwell to death without a trial and he was beheaded at the Tower of London on 28 July 1540 – the same day Henry VIII married his fifth queen, Catherine Howard.

Althoughe the dystaunce of tyme and accompte of dayes nether be so
longe nor many of your maiesties absens, yett the wounte of your present so muche
beloved and desired of me, the wante therof maketh me that I can not quyetly
pleasure in any thynge vntyll I here from your maiestye: the tyme therfor
semeth to me very longe, wythe a grett desire to knowe how your
highnes hathe done syns your departynge hense, whose prosperite and
helthe I prefer and desyre more then myne owne. And wheras I
knowe your maiesties absens ys neuer wythe out grett respectes of thynges
most convenyent and necessary, yett love and affection compelleth me to
desyre your present: And agayne the same zele and love forceth me
also to be best content wythe that whiche ys your wyll and pleasure: And
thus love maketh me in all thynges to sett apart myne owne comodite
and pleasure, and to embrase most joyfully hys wyll and pleasure whom
I love. God the knower of secretes can juge these wordes not to be only
wrytten wythe ynke, but most truely imprissed in the hert, muche more
I omytte, lest I sholde seme to go abonte to prayse my self, or crave a
thanke, wyche thynge to do I mynde nothyng lesse, but playne symple
relacyon of my zele and love towarde your maiestye procedyng from
the abundance of the herte, wherin I must nedes confesse I desire no
worthye comendation, havyng suche juste occasion to do the same
I make lyke accompte wythe your maiestye, as I do wythe god for hys
benefytes and gyftes heped vpon me dayly, knowledgyng my self all
wayes a grette detter vnto hym in that I do omytt my dutye towarde
hym, nott being able to recompense the leste of hys benefytes, in wyche
state I am certeyne and sure to dye, but yett I hope in hys gracyous acceptation of my good wyll. And even suche confidence I have in your maiesties gentylnes, knowyng my self neuer to have done my dutye as
were requysite and mete to suche a noble and worthy prynce, at whose
handes I have founde and received so muche love and goodnes that wythe
wordes I can not expresse yt: lest I sholde be to tedyouse vnto your maiestye
I fynyshe thys my screbeled letter, comyttyng you in to the governance of the lorde
wt long lyfe and prosperouse felycite here, & after thys lyfe to enioy the kyngdome of hys
electe. from grenewyche

by your maiesties humble and
obedient lovyng wyfe and
seruant Katheryn the Quene KP

Catherine Howard and Katherine Parr

Autograph letter by Katherine Parr, to Henry VIII, pleading for news of his military expedition in France. Greenwich, [July 1544].

British Library, Lansdowne MS 1236, f. 9

Although the discourse of time and account of days neither is long nor many of Your Majesty's absence, yet the want of your presence, so much beloved and desired of me, maketh me that I cannot quietly pleasure in anything until I hear from your Majesty. The time, therefore, seemeth to me very long, with a great desire to know how your Highness hath done since your departing hence, whose prosperity and health I prefer and desire more than mine own. And whereas I know your Majesty's absence is never without great respects of things most convenient and necessary, yet love and affection compelleth me to desire your presence. And again, the same zeal and love forces me also to be best content with that which is your will and pleasure. And thus love maketh me in all things to set apart mine one commodity and pleasure and to embrace most joyfully his will and pleasure whom I love. God, the knower of secrets, can judge these words not to be only written with ink, but most truly impressed in the heart. Much more I omit, lest I should seem to go about to praise myself, or crave a thank, which thing to do I mind nothing less, but a plain, simple relation of my zeal and love toward your Majesty, proceeding from the abundance of the heart. Wherein I must needs confess I deserve no worthy commendation, having such just occasion to do the same. I make like account with your Majesty as I do with God for his benefits and gifts heaped upon me daily, acknowledging myself always a great debtor unto him in that I do omit my duty toward him, not being able to recompense the least of his benefits; in which state I am certain and sure to die, but yet I hope in his gracious acceptation of my goodwill. And even such confidence I have in your Majesty's gentleness, knowing myself never to have done my duty as was requisite and mete to such a noble and worthy prince, at whose hands I have found and received so much love and goodness, that with words I cannot express it. Lest I should be too tedious unto your Majesty, I finish this my scribbled letter, committing you into the governance of the Lord with long life and prosperous felicity here, and after this life to enjoy the kingdom of his elect. From Greenwich.

By your Majesty's humble obedient loving wife and servant,

Katherine the queen. KP.

C atherine Howard, the attractive and vivacious niece of Thomas Howard, Duke of Norfolk, and a cousin of Anne Boleyn, caught the King's eye when she entered Anne of Cleves' household as a maid of honour. Despite being thirty years her senior, by the spring of 1540 Henry had taken Catherine as his mistress and married her on 28 July 1540. Catherine was sexually experienced beyond her teenage years and, unlike Anne of Cleves, knew how to please the ageing King. Henry was besotted and daily lavished gifts of precious gems on Catherine. After spending the summer of 1541 together on royal progress in the north of England, Henry ordered public thanksgiving for his marriage to be made on All Saints' Day (1 November). The next day, as Henry attended Mass, Archbishop Thomas Cranmer passed him a note containing details of Catherine's pre-marital sexual relationships with her music tutor, Henry Mannox, and the Tudor courtier Francis Dereham. Henry initially refused to believe the allegations, but further investigation confirmed them to be true and furthermore revealed that, as Queen, Catherine had enjoyed reckless nocturnal assignations with Thomas Culpeper, a Gentleman of the King's Household and royal favourite. On 22 November 1541, Catherine was stripped of her title of Queen and two days later she was charged with having led 'an abominable, base, carnal, voluptuous and vicious life' before marrying Henry and deceiving him since with an 'outward appearance of chastity and honesty'. She was executed on 13 February 1542, and Henry, left heartbroken and humiliated by Catherine's infidelity, did not marry again for over a year.

For his sixth wife, the King chose more appropriately. On 12 July 1543, he married the twice-widowed Katherine Parr in the Queen's Closet at Hampton Court in the presence of his children Mary, Elizabeth and Edward. Henry was not Katherine's preferred choice of husband; she was already in love with the younger, more exciting Thomas Seymour, brother of Jane Seymour. Nevertheless, Katherine nobly put duty before love and became Henry's sixth and final queen consort. Famous for being the wife who 'survived' Henry, Katherine's true significance was her influence on his family. She was a loving stepmother and helped to establish a better relationship between Henry and his children, with the result that, for the first time, the King's family enjoyed some stability and harmony. Katherine is also widely credited with persuading Henry to restore Mary and Elizabeth to the succession in 1543, and she provided her stepdaughters with a strong model of queenship. Well educated and fluent in French, Latin and Italian, Katherine enjoyed reading Petrarch and Erasmus and she was also the first Queen of England to have her own work published when *Prayers or Meditations* – a collection of English devotional material and prayers – appeared in her name on 29 May 1549. Katherine's interest in learning became an important part of her relationship with her stepchildren as she inspired and encouraged each of her stepchildren in their intellectual pursuits, as evidenced by their surviving correspondence, written in French, Italian, Latin and English.

In July 1544, Henry sought military glory on the international stage for the last time, personally leading the siege of Boulogne as part of a joint Anglo–Habsburg invasion of France. Before setting sail, Henry appointed Katherine his Queen Regent-General during his absence. Katherine's touching letter to Henry, written shortly after his departure, indicates that their marriage was very loving and affectionate, and it conveys a strong sense of the comfort and companionship that she provided Henry during his final years. Full of heartfelt pleas for news of the King, Katherine's letter tells him that, even though she understands his absence is necessary, 'love and affection compelleth me to desire your presence'. In the final section of the letter Katherine reveals her radical religious beliefs which, two years later, nearly led to her arrest for heresy during a conservative plot to rid the court of prominent evangelicals. Katherine finishes the letter by comparing her love for Henry with her love for God. Daringly, she does so by expounding the Lutheran belief that faith alone, without the necessity of good works, was sufficient for salvation. Katherine acknowledged herself 'a great debtor' unto God and unable to 'recompense the least of his benefits'. She was 'certain and sure to die' in this condition of sinfulness and yet she was confident of God's gracious acceptance of her 'goodwill' (faith) and his forgiveness of her sins. Katherine was, she explained, equally confident of Henry's continued 'gentleness' towards her even though she could never repay his abundant 'love and goodness'.

KING
EDWARD VI.

EDWARD VI

After the death of king henry theight his son edward prince of wea
was come to at hartford by therle of hertford and f anthony
brown master of thorse to for whom befor was made great
preparacon that he might created prince of wales, and after
ward was brought to Infild Whear the death of his father
was first shewed him, and the same day the death of
his father was shewed in London Wher was great
lamentation and weping and sodenly he proclaimed king
the next day being the   of   he was brought to
the towre of London Whear he taried thespace of three wke
and in the mean season the counsel sat euery day for the
pformaunce of the will and at lenght thought best that
the Erle of Hartford shuld be made duc of Somerset
the lord Adele f Thomas seimour L Sudley. The erle of
Essex Marquis of Northampton and diuers other knigh
should be mad Barons as the L Sheffield to diuers
other Also thei thought best to chose the duke
of Somerset to be protectour of the realm and govr
nor of the kinges person to wich during his men
to wich al the gentlemen and Lordes did agre becaus
he was the kinges oncle on his mothers side Also
in this time the late king was buried at windsor
to much solemnite and thofficers broke thear staues
hurling them into the graue. But thei wer restored
to them again when thei came to the towre the
on of warwic also was m L isle was mad
erle of warwic and the lord Chamberlain after ship
was giuen to him and the L Sudley mad
admirall of England. Al this thinges wer don
the king being in the towre. Afterward al
thinges being prepared for the corronacon the
king being then but nin yere old passed through
the cite of London and as hiertofore hath beni used
and cam to the palace if westminster and the
next day cam into westminster hal and ther
asked the peple whether thei wold haue him to

The Death of Henry VIII and Accession of Edward VI

The first page of Edward VI's autograph 'Chronicle' or diary, in which he records the death of his father, King Henry VIII. 1547?.

British Library, Cotton MS Nero C x, f. 12

After the death of King Henry the Eighth, his son Edward, Prince of Wales, was come to at Hertford by the Earl of Hertford and Sir Anthony Browne, Master of the Horse, for whom before was made great preparation that he might [be] created Prince of Wales, and afterward was brought to Enfield, where the death of his father was first showed him, and the same day the death of his father was showed in London, where [there] was great lamentation and weeping; and suddenly he [was] proclaimed King. The next day, being the [31st] of [January] he was brought to the Tower of London, where he tarried the space of three weeks; and in the mean season the Council sat every day for the performance of the will and at length thought best that the Earl of Hertford should be made Duke of Somerset, Sir Thomas Seymour Lord Sudeley, the Earl of Essex Marquis of Northampton, and divers knights should be made barons, as the Lord Sheffield, with divers other[s]. Also they thought best to choose the Duke of Somerset to be Protector of the realm and Governor of the King's person during his minority, to which all the gentlemen and lords did agree, because he was the King's uncle on his mother's side. Also in this time the late King was buried at Windsor with much solemnity, and the officers broke their staves hurling them into the grave. But they were restored to them again when they came to the Tower. The Lord Lisle was made Earl of Warwick, and the lord great chamberlainship was given to him; and the Lord Sudeley [was] made Admiral of England.

All these things were done, the King being in the Tower. Afterward, all things being prepared for the coronation, the King, being then but nine years old, passed through the City of London as heretofore hath been used, and came to the palace of Westminster, and the next day came into Westminster Hall, and it was asked [of] the people whether they would have him to be their King, who answered 'Yea, yea'.

Henry VIII's physical health became a growing cause for concern following a near-disastrous fall that terminated his jousting career in 1536. Over the next decade the King was plagued by illness and suffered frequent headaches, bouts of fever and painful ulcers in his legs as a result of jousting injuries. As the 1540s wore on, Henry's obesity left him increasingly immobile, requiring him to be carried about his palaces in a specially constructed form of chair. The transformation from the slim, handsome, athletic, golden prince to the bloated, pain-ridden and anxious old king is nowhere more vividly summed up than in Henry's personal Psalter, where, next to a verse in Psalm 36 which reads, 'I have been young and now am old,' Henry wrote *dolens dictum* (a sad saying).

By December 1546 it was obvious that Henry was dying and Queen Katherine was sent to Greenwich Palace for Christmas while he remained at Whitehall. On 26 December the King revised his will. Dated 30 December 1546 and signed using the dry-stamp (a form of signature by proxy which he had introduced in 1545), it made provisions for a Regency Council to govern the realm until Edward reached maturity. The sixteen councillors appointed by the King were predominantly supporters of the reformed religion and included Edward's godfather, Archbishop Thomas Cranmer; Edward's maternal uncle, Edward Seymour; the Queen's brother, William Parr; John Dudley, son of Henry VII's hated enforcer Edmund Dudley; Sir William Paget, the King's secretary; and Thomas Wriothesley, the King's Lord Chancellor and the only prominent conservative among the sixteen. Henry intended the Council to rule collectively, by majority decision, with 'like and equal charge', and so made no provision for the appointment of a Protector.

After Henry died at Whitehall Palace in the early hours of Friday 28 January 1547, the arrangements he had put in place for Edward's minority soon started to unravel. News of the King's death was kept secret for three days while Edward Seymour and his main supporter, Sir William Paget, plotted to take control of the young King and the Council. As Edward would later record in his *Chronicle*, in his boyishly untidy hand, it was Seymour (the then Earl of Hertford) who rode to the medieval palace of Hertford to take him to his sister Elizabeth's residence at the palace of Enfield, where the two children were informed of their father's death. Edward and Elizabeth are said to have wept in each other's arms, but, frustratingly, Edward recorded nothing of his personal feelings in his *Chronicle*, focusing instead on the political and military events of his reign. What we are left with is his rather detached observation that Henry's death caused 'great lamentation and weeping' in London.

On Monday 31 January, Henry's death was officially announced in Parliament and the nine-year-old Edward was proclaimed King Edward VI. Later that same day, the Regency Council convened at the Tower of London and nominated Edward Seymour as Lord Protector of England and Governor of Edward's person. Over the next few days Seymour and his allies awarded themselves lands and titles: Edward Seymour himself was elevated to the Dukedom of Somerset, the family title of the Beauforts, through whom Henry VII had claimed his right to the throne; John Dudley became the Earl of Warwick; William Parr was created Marquis of Northampton and Thomas Wriothesley was made Earl of Southampton. Edward Seymour's brother, Thomas, was added to the Regency Council and created Baron Seymour of Sudeley. As Queen of England for four years and Regent-General in 1544, Katherine Parr had every reason to expect to participate in the regency but, contrary to her expectation, she was excluded from power. When she married her true love, Thomas Seymour, just months after Henry's death, she relinquished any influence she might have had and alienated Edward. Tragically, Katherine would die the following year, shortly after giving birth to her first child, a daughter, whom she named Mary after her eldest stepdaughter.

Henry VIII was laid to rest on 15 February 1547 in the vault of St George's Chapel at Windsor Castle alongside Jane Seymour, Edward's mother and Henry's favourite queen. On Saturday 19 February, Edward made his formal entry into London, riding from the Tower of London in a grand procession to Westminster Palace. He was crowned king the following day in Westminster Abbey. Edward dutifully read out the coronation oath, which had been amended by Cranmer to make it clear that the crown held imperial jurisdiction over the Church and that it would use the Royal Supremacy to drive forward the Reformation. In his coronation address, Cranmer reminded Edward that he was now 'God's Vicegerent and Christ's Vicar' within his dominions, and exhorted him to emulate Josiah, the boy-king who, in the Old Testament, had ordered the destruction of idolatry and images in Israel.

Derest Vncle by your lettres and reporte of the messenger, we haue at good length Vnderstande
to our great comfort, the good succese, it hathe ~~yet~~ pleased god to graunte Vs against the Scottes by
your good courage and wise forsight, for the wich and other the benefites of god, heaped Vpon vs,
like as we ar most bounden to yeld him most humble thankes, and to seke bi al waies we m
his true honour, So do we giue Vnto you, good Vncle our most hartie thankes, praying you to th
also most hartelie in our name our good Cosin there of Warwike, and all the othere of the nob
gentlemen, and others that haue serued in this iournei, of whose seruice they shall all be well
assured, we will not (god graunte vs lief) shew our selfes Vnmindfull, but be redy euer to co
the same as anie occasion shall serue. yeuen at our house of Oetlandes, the eighteneth of Septem
ber.

your good neuew

Edward

War Against Scotland

Autograph letter by Edward VI, to Edward Seymour, the Duke of
Somerset, Lord Protector, congratulating him on the English victory
at the Battle of Pinkie Cleugh. 18 September 1547.
British Library, Lansdowne MS 1236, f. 16

*Dearest uncle, by your letters and report of the messenger, we have at good length
understanded, to our great comfort, the good success it hath pleased God to grant us against
the Scots by your good courage and wise foresight, for the which and other the benefits of
God heaped upon us, like as we are most bounden to yield him most humble thanks, and
to seek by all ways we may, his true honour. So do we give unto you, good uncle, our most
hearty thanks, praying you to thank also most heartily, in our name, our good cousin the
Earl of Warwick, and all the other of the noblemen, gentlemen, and others, that have
served in this journey, of whose service they shall all be well assured, we will not (God
grant us life) show ourselves unmindful, but be ready ever to consider the same as any
occasion shall serve. Given at our house of Oatlands, the eighteenth of September,*

Your good nephew,
Edward.

In 1547, England was diplomatically and religiously isolated and the new government of Edward Seymour, Duke of Somerset, faced several threatening foreign situations. In April of that year, the Holy Roman Emperor, Charles V, defeated the German Protestants at the Battle of Mühlberg, which was a major setback for Protestant power in Europe. Scotland was still smarting from its resounding defeat by the English army at the Battle of Solway Moss on 24 November 1542, Henry VIII having invaded to secure his northern borders before returning to war against France. Henry II, the new and militarily aggressive King of France, was determined to win back the strategically important port of Boulogne, captured by Henry VIII in 1544. Moreover, the accession of Henry II saw the Guise family return to a position of power and influence in France. The sudden death of James V, days after Scotland's catastrophic defeat at Solway Moss, made it almost inevitable that Maire of Guise, his formidable widow and mother of the infant Mary Stuart, Queen of Scotland, would look for opportunities to strengthen Scotland's 'Auld Alliance' with France.

After the English victory at Solway Moss and the death of James V, Henry VIII had in fact tried to weaken French influence in Scotland once and for all by arranging the betrothal of Mary Stuart to his son, Prince Edward, in order to unite England and Scotland and impose the Anglican Reformation on the Scottish Church. The terms of marriage were confirmed by the Treaty of Greenwich, which was signed on 1 July 1543 but quickly repudiated by the Scottish Parliament. Henry was furious and in spring 1544 he ordered a campaign of military harassment known as the 'Rough Wooing', which was intended to force the Scots into a change of policy, but instead strengthened the traditional Franco-Scottish alliance.

Several raids had been led by Edward Seymour, who, on 10 April, had been instructed by Henry's Privy Council to 'Put all to fire and sword, burn Edinburgh, so razed and defaced when you have sacked and gotten what ye can of it, as there may remain forever a perpetual memory of the vengeance of God lightened upon (them) for their falsehood and disloyalty'. Seymour was one of the King's most accomplished military leaders and he did what was asked of him, almost totally destroying Edinburgh and Holyrood and setting ablaze hundreds of Scottish towns and villages. On 18 May, he wrote to Henry to inform him that 'this journey is accomplished to your Majesty's honour, in such sort as we trust your Majesty shall hear talk the like devastation hath not been made in Scotland these many years'. Henry was delighted, but chose to ignore Seymour's advice to garrison and occupy strategic parts of Scotland.

In 1547, Seymour's new status as Lord Protector of England and Duke of Somerset provided him with the opportunity to renew war against Scotland and implement his garrisoning policy. This time the military campaign was accompanied by a propaganda drive to persuade the Scots of the benefits of uniting the two kingdoms to form 'one island of Great Britain' and Somerset himself penned an *Epistle to Unity and Peace* for circulation in Scotland. In August 1547, English forces crossed the border, accompanied along the coast by a number of warships. On 10 September, the Battle of Pinkie Cleugh, which would prove to be the last pitched battle between Scottish and English armies, took place near Musselburgh, east of Edinburgh. Despite being outnumbered, the English soldiers, equipped with state-of-the-art weaponry and supported by sea-based artillery, inflicted a crushing defeat on the Scottish forces. Somerset immediately seized and garrisoned a number of Scottish castles in the Lowlands, his plan being to conquer the country and compel the Scots to agree to the marriage of King Edward VI and Mary, Queen of Scots, and the union of the two crowns.

Like his father before him, Edward VI showed great enthusiasm for warfare and he wrote this letter of congratulations and appreciation to Somerset after learning of the English victory at Pinkie Cleugh. What Edward could not have realized at the time was that Somerset had achieved a hollow victory, for the Scottish campaign would ultimately achieve nothing. In June 1548, French troops arrived in Scotland to help to repel the English enemy and Somerset's garrisoning policy proved to be both futile and a huge financial drain on the economy. The English cause in Scotland was completely lost when, on 7 August 1548, the five-year-old Queen Mary was smuggled out of Scotland to France. She would later marry the *dauphin* Francis, who, in 1559, would become King Francis II. To make matters worse, on 8 August 1549 King Henry II declared war on England and French troops laid siege to Boulogne, which was surrendered the following year.

ses preceptes cest a dire adorer
des images offrir aux Idoles et diable
il nous brusle et nous fait porter
un fagot: ou quel ces f gehenne et
tormente. Aux iours du mon pere
quand son nom estoit oblittere en
des liures il estouppa les bouches de
Chrestiens auec ses six articles come
auec six points. Aussy maintena
en france deuant que quelquune
brusle ils ostent sa langue, a cette
afin quil ne parlast veu donques
que le pape est le ministre a
Lucifer iay bon espoir que com
Lucifer tomboit hors du ciel en
enfer aynsy que le pape son vicaire
tombera hors de ceste gloire de
la papaulte en grande derision.

ar Dauid dit aux Psaulmes que dieu   Psal. 12
eut estre puers auec les puers   C
& sainct auec les saincts. Mais Or
pape a auite l'honneur de dieu
pourtant que iay bon espoir que dieu
y neult auter ses honneurs et sa gloi=
re. Aussy Marie a dit que dieu   Luc. 1
m a auite la gloire des riches et
a donnee aux humbles. Pourtant
pape se gardes bien, Car si
u tombes tu auras une grande chute,
et tout aynsy quun homme qui est
monte en une tour sil tumbe ail
aura une grande cheute aynsy
ui auez montes iusques aux cieux
mberez iusques a l'enfer, aynsy que Matt. 11
rist predit de Tyr et sidon.   d
Mais pour venir a la ... du

A Second Josiah

An opening from Edward VI's autograph draft of his treatise against
the papal supremacy, completed in 1549 and dedicated to his uncle, Edward
Seymour, the Duke of Somerset, Lord Protector.

British Library, Additional MS 5464, ff. 26v–27

Let us therefore see whether the Pope be the minister of God or the devil; which I fear he
will prove; proclaiming himself a good man, a most holy bishop, a king of kings; whereas
he is the tyrant of tyrants; all others exercising their tyranny over bodies, but this devil,
wolf, tyrant, exercises his tyranny over the souls of men, constraining the poor and simple
lambs of God to forsake their faith, whereby they are saved, to follow his abominable
traditions and diabolical precepts; which if they refuse to obey, to wit, adoring images,
and offering to his idols and devils, he burns, racks, and torments them, or forces them to
a costly recantation. During the reign of my late father the King, when the Pope's name
was blotted out of our books, he stopped the mouths of Christians with his Six Articles,
as if he would choke them.

 And at this day in France, before any one is burnt, a little before the execution, they cut
out his tongue, that they might not speak. Considering then that the Pope is the minister
of Lucifer, I am in good hopes, that as Lucifer fell from heaven into hell, so the Pope, his
vicar, will fall from the great glory of the papacy into contemptible derision. For David
hath said (Ps. 18) in the Psalms, With the pure thou wilt shew thyself pure, and
with the froward thou wilt shew thyself froward. *Again, the Pope hath taken*
God's honour away from him; therefore, I hope, God will divest him of his honours and
glory. As Mary the mother of Jesus saith (Luke 1) He hath put down the mighty
from their seats, and exalted them of low degree. *Take heed of thyself, then, O*
Pope, for if thou tumblest, thou wilt have a terrible fall. As a man who has got up into
a high tower would have a huge leap if he should fall down, so thou who hast exalted
thyself into the heavens, would fall down into the abyss of hell, as Christ foretold of Tyre
and Sidon (Matt. 11). But to return to the Pope's primacy. I know very well that the
Scripture speaks of one God, one faith, one baptism (Eph. 4; 1 Cor. 8; 1 Tim. 2; Matt.
19.) but no mention of one Pope.

Unlike Henry VII and Henry VIII, Edward VI was born to rule and so was groomed for kingship from an early age, receiving the best and most extensive education that money could buy. His first tutor was the Cambridge-educated headmaster of Eton, Dr Richard Cox, who was appointed in July 1544. He was assisted by Sir John Cheke, first Regius Professor of Greek at Oxford, who taught Edward Greek and Latin; Princess Elizabeth's tutor Roger Ascham; and Jean Belmaine, a French Huguenot, who taught Edward his language. From an early age, Edward showed great intellectual ability and was a diligent and talented student, prompting Richard Cox to write to Edward's godfather, Archbishop Thomas Cranmer, that he:

was of such towardness in learning, godliness, gentleness and all honest qualities, that both you and I and all this realm ought to think him and take him for a singular gift sent of God, an imp worthy of such a father; for whom we are bound without ceasing to render to God most hearty thanks, with most humble request of his long and prosperous continuance. He hath learned almost four books of Cato to construe, to parse, and to say without book. And of his own courage now, in the latter book, he will needs have at one time fourteen verses, which he conneth pleasantly and perfectly, besides things of the Bible, Satellitium Vivis, Æsop's Fables, and Latin-making, whereof he hath sent your Grace a little taste.

Significantly, all of Edward's tutors were committed to evangelical reform. As a result of their guidance and the influence of Katherine Parr and Cranmer, Edward already held strong evangelical views by the time he became king, and he advocated a full-scale Protestant Reformation in England. Edward's schoolwork provides striking evidence of his evangelical enthusiasm and reforming zeal. His commitment to the Royal Supremacy is fully apparent in this, his anti-papal treatise, which he began to compose in December 1548 at the age of eleven. Shown here is a page of an early draft, written in French in Edward's own hand and corrected in places by Jean Belmaine, who set the young prince such exercises not only to advance his French, but also to teach him to defend key doctrines of his reformed English Church.

The evangelical establishment around Edward, led by the Lord Protector and Cranmer, immediately began to accelerate religious change to move the English people towards Protestantism and away from Henry VIII's religious orthodoxy and 'middle way'. As an immediate concession to evangelicals, Parliament repealed the Act of Six Articles of 1539 and lifted restrictions on the printing of Protestant literature and reading the Bible. In July 1547, Cranmer published his official *Book of Homilies*, a collection of sermons that expounded the Protestant doctrine of justification by faith alone. The *Homilies* were intended for use throughout the Church of England and were imposed upon the clergy by a radical new set of royal injunctions issued on 31 July 1547, which set out plans for the dismantling of traditional religion. Clergy were instructed to destroy all imagery in churches and, over the next two years, much of English and Welsh medieval religious art was lost as the injunctions were enforced by commissioners: holy statues were smashed, stained-glass windows broken and wall paintings whitewashed. The injunctions also forbade the burning of all candles, except for two placed on the altar, and they banned the use of rosary beads and holy water. Legislation dissolving the chantries, where Masses were sung for the souls of the deceased, was also approved on the grounds that belief in Purgatory and prayers for the dead were superstitious. The following year, Cranmer began to impose further liturgical changes that would radically alter the laity's experience of church services. A new vernacular Order of the Communion meant that the Latin Mass was now to be said in English, and, in a dramatic break from Catholic tradition, wine as well as bread was to be administered to the laity, thus enabling them to fully participate in the Communion service for the first time. On Whit Sunday, 9 June 1549, Cranmer's *Book of Common Prayer* was enforced by an Act of Uniformity as the only legal form of worship in England. The book provided new reformed liturgy for the services of 'the Holy Communion commonly called the Mass', Matins, Evensong, baptism, confirmation and marriage. Many of Cranmer's evangelical allies were disappointed that the new service book was not more radical or explicitly Protestant, but for the English people, it marked a dramatic break with the past, for all religious services were henceforth to be held in English instead of Latin.

Most people accepted the *Book of Common Prayer* but in Cornwall and Devon it sparked significant uprisings, known as the Western Rebellion. The rebels demanded a return to their old religion, the reinstatement of the Act of Six Articles and in particular the restoration of the Latin Mass and other traditional liturgical ceremonies. Thousands of Devon and Cornish rebels united and marched on Exeter and laid siege to the city. The government lost control of the area for about two months until the uprising was ruthlessly suppressed by John Russell, Earl of Bedford.

The Downfall of
Lord Protector Somerset

Letter signed by Lords of the Council in London, to the Council at
Windsor, declaring their intention to remove Edward Seymour, the Duke of
Somerset, from the Protectorship. London, 7 October 1549.

British Library, Cotton MS Caligula B vii, f. 415r–v

*My Lords, after our right hearty commendations, understanding what false, untrue, and
slanderous bills, rumours, and reports be spread in many places, by means of the Duke of
Somerset and his adherents, of the cause of our assembly; and being together, we have first
thought good, to assure your Lordships of our honours, truth, and fidelities to God and
the King's Majesty, that we mean nothing else but the surety of his Majesty's person, our
most gracious Sovereign Lord, the preservation of his honour, and the good governance of
his Majesty's realms and dominions; and, for none other cause, we take God to witness.
If the Duke of Somerset would at any time have heard our advices, if he would have
heard reason, and [ac]knowledged himself a subject, our meanings was to have quietly
communed with him for redress of all things without any disturbance of the realm; but
knowing afterwards that the said Duke goeth about to raise great forces and numbers of
men, to spread abroad slanderous and untrue reports of us much contrary to our honours
and reputations, we were forced for the meeting therewith, against our wills to assemble
also some numbers about us. And now touching the matter, like as it grieveth us to see
what danger and peril may ensue to the whole realm through division amongst ourselves,
we have likewise thought good to signify unto you that if the said Duke will, as becometh
a good subject absent himself from his Majesty, be contented to be ordered according to
justice and reason, and disperse that force which is levied by him, we will gladly commune
with you touching the surety of his Majesty's person, and order of all other things, wherein
we nothing doubt, whatsoever hath been otherwise untruly reported, you shall find us
both conformable and ready to do as becometh good subjects and true councillors; nothing
doubting to find the like conformity also on your behalves. Otherwise, if we shall see that
you mind more the maintenance of that one man's ill doings than the execution of his
Majesty's laws and common order, we must make other accompt [account] of you than we
trust we shall have cause.*

Consider my Lords, for God's sake, we heartily pray you, that we be almost the whole Council, men that have been too much bounden by sundry benefits to forget our duties to the King's Majesty, for whom we do that we do, and will gladly spend our lives for his surety. If you forsake to come to this good and peaceable agreement, we must protest that the inconveniences which may ensue upon stir must grow of you, the danger whereof we assuredly know is to none of you unknown. Thus praying God to send us and your grace to do that may most conduce to his glory and wealth of the Realm. We bid you heartily farewell. From London this viith of October 1549.

Your assured loving friends

Richard Rich
Chancellor

William Lord Saint John

William Parr,
Marquis of Northampton

John Dudley,
Earl of Warwick

Henry Fitzalan,
Earl of Arundel

Francis Talbot,
Earl of Shrewsbury

Thomas Wriothesley, Earl of Southampton

Sir Thomas Cheyne

Sir William Petre

Sir Edward North

Sir John Gage

Sir Ralph Sadleir

Sir Richard Southwell

Dr Nicholas Wotton

My lorde After o[ur] right harti comend[aci]ons vnderstand
what false vntrue and slanderous b[i]lle rumo[rs] and repp[ortes]
be spred in many place by meanes of the duke of Somset &
his adherens of the cause of o[ur] assemble and being togi[ther]
we have first thought good t[o]assure yo[ur] lordships of o[ur]
honour[s] truthe and fidelitie to god and the kinge ma[jes]tie
we mean nothing elle but the sewrtie of his ma[jes]tie so
o[ur] most graciou[s] sou[er]aign lord, the p[re]s[er]vacion of his hig[h]
and the good gou[er]naunce of his ma[jes]tie realme and dom[inions]
and for none other cause we take god to witnes, if the[y]
of Somset wold at any tyme have hard o[ur] advise,
he wold have hard reason and knowlege himselfe a sut[or]
o[ur] meaninge was to have quietly remaued w[ith] him so
redresse of all thinge w[ith]out any distourbaunce of the rea[lm]
but knowing afterwards that the said duke goethe about
w[ith] great forse and nombers of men, to spredd abrode slander
and vntrue reporte, of w[hiche] more contrary to o[ur] honos and repp[orts]
trous, we were forced for the metyng therin aga[i]nst o[ur] will
t[o]assemble alsso some nombers about vs And now tou[ching] th[e]
mater, w[hi]ch ab[ov]e p[ro]bable it[t] is to see what daunger and p[er]ill
may ensue to these realme thorough diuision amongst o[ur]selfe
we have lykewise thought good to signifie vnto you that
if the said duke will ab b[e]co[m]eth a good subiect absent
himselfe from his ma[jes]tie, be content to be ordered according
to iustice and reason, and disperse that forse w[hi]ch he hath
aby him we will gladly cou[m] w[ith] you tou[ching] the sew[rtie]
of his ma[jes]tie p[er]son and order of all other thinge wher[in]
nothing doubt what soeuer have they otherwise vntrue
reported you shall fynd vs bothe conformable and redy
to do as b[e]co[m]eth good subiecte and tru[e] cou[n]sellors nothing
doubting to fynd the like conformitie alsso on yo[ur] behalfe
otherwise if we shall see that you mynde more the ma[in]
tenance of that one mans ill doing then the[n] honour[s]
of his ma[jes]tie lawes and comen order we must make oth[er]
accompt of you then we trust we shall have cause

BRITISH MUSEUM

Consider my Lorde for goddes sake we hartely pray you that
we be almost the hole counsell, who that have byn to morthe
bounden by sundry benefite to forgett owr duties to the Kynge
maies for whom we do that we do and will gladly spend
owr lyffes to his service / if you forsake to come to this
good and peaceable agrement, we must protest that the
mischeimentes which may ensue thereof must growe of you
the daunger whereof we assuredly know is to none of you
unknowen / Thus praying god to stand us and you grace
to do that may most redue to his glorie & wealth of
the realme we byd you hartely fare well. ffrom
London the vijth octobr 1549

yor assured loving freendes

[Signatures:]

Thomas Cheyne   John   W. Northt
J Barwyke   Arundell   T Shrewesbury

                    Hnry Sonthampton

    T Cheyne   William peter   Edward Rozth

  John Gage

  Ser Southwell   R Sadler
                                    Nicholas Wotton

Lord Protector Somerset's disastrous Scottish campaign compounded the severe financial problems created by Henry VIII's wars of the 1540s against France and Scotland, with the result that, by 1549, the Exchequer was almost bankrupt. Royal debt led to renewed plundering of Church wealth, this time through the sale of chantries, and further debasement of English coinage, which, in turn, caused inflation. Unfortunately for Somerset, while the Western Rebellion was being suppressed, another mass uprising broke out in Norfolk, which quickly spread across East Anglia under the leadership of local yeoman farmer Robert Kett. Unlike the Western Rebellion, Kett's uprising was triggered by social and economic grievances. Soaring inflation, rising rents and food prices and increased taxes had worsened the plight of the poor in the region. In particular, the enclosure of common lands by the landowning gentry for sheep grazing resulted in the poor being driven off the land that they relied upon to feed their families when paid work dried up. Somerset was sympathetic to their plight and set up enclosure commissions to enforce existing anti-enclosure statutes. However, the policy was a failure, as were attempts to introduce a new law against enclosure, and the commoners grew increasingly frustrated.

Initially, the country-folk of East Anglia who participated in Kett's rebellion set up peaceful protest camps throughout Norfolk and Suffolk and sent their demands – no enclosure, no debasement and lower rents – to Somerset and their local gentry. At first, Somerset ignored his fellow councillors' advice to use force and instead tried to negotiate with the rebels, promising a pardon to all those 'rude and ignorant people' who had 'riotously assembled themselves', on condition that they disbanded. When Kett and his followers launched an attack on the city of Norwich, John Dudley, Earl of Warwick, was sent to suppress the rebellion and, on 27 August 1549, a full-scale battle took place at Dussindale, southwest of Norwich. It is estimated that 3,500 of Kett's men lost their lives and Kett himself was captured, convicted of treason, and hanged from the battlements of Norwich Castle on 7 December.

By the autumn of 1549, Somerset's ruinous foreign and social policies and his arrogant and autocratic style of leadership had alienated the majority of his colleagues on the Privy Council. Warwick's successful defeat of Kett's Norfolk rebellion made him the obvious choice to replace Somerset, who was at Hampton Court with the King when he realized that Warwick was plotting against him. Edward VI later recorded in his *Chronicle* that Somerset 'commanded the armour to be brought out of the armoury of Hampton Court, about 500 harnesses, to arm both his and my men with it, the gates of the house to be fortified, and people to be raised'. That night Somerset fled with Edward to Windsor Castle, where he made an unsuccessful appeal to the people to 'aid the King against the Lords'. A stand-off ensued between the Lords of the Council in London and Somerset, who had been joined at Windsor by Archbishop Thomas Cranmer, Secretary Thomas Smith and Sir William Paget. This dramatic letter, sent by Warwick and the other London councillors to the Council at Windsor, outlines their grievances against Somerset and expresses their concern for the 'surety of his Majesty's person'. It strongly warned Cranmer, Paget and Smith not to 'mind more the maintenance of that one man's ill doings than the execution of his Majesty's laws and common order' and urged them to come to a 'good and peaceable agreement'. Cranmer, who had been Somerset's closest and most loyal ally, persuaded him to surrender on 11 October. The Protectorate was dissolved on 13 October and Somerset, indicted for 'ambition, vainglory and entering into rash wars', was imprisoned in the Tower of London. A fierce struggle for power ensued between the religious conservatives (who, led by Thomas Wriothesley, Earl of Southampton, wanted to make the Lady Mary Regent for her brother King Edward and return England to Catholicism) and the evangelical councillors, with Warwick, backed by Cranmer and William Paget, as their leader. The struggle was won by Warwick, who, in January 1550, was appointed Lord President of the Privy Council and in October 1551 had himself created Duke of Northumberland.

The Duke of Somerset was released from the Tower in January 1550 and readmitted to the Privy Council soon after, although he never regained serious influence. Warwick kept a close eye on his rival, and two years later, when he discovered that Somerset was plotting to topple him, ordered his re-arrest and execution. Without any hint of emotion, Edward VI recorded in his *Chronicle* that on 22 January 1552 his uncle 'the Duke of Somerset had his head cut off upon Tower Hill between eight and nine o'clock in the morning.'

It is no small greyf to me to parceyve / that they / whom the
ma.te my father / whose soule god pardon) made in thys worlde o
nothyng in respecte of that they be come to nowe / and at hys laste
put in truste to se hys wyll parfourmed / whereunto they w
for the love z feare to theym (bothe howe they breake har in
all sworne vpon a boke / it greyueth me J say to se what vn
power they take vpon theym / in makyng (as they call it) law
both cleane contrarye to hys procedyngs z wyll / and also agaynst
the custome of all crystendome / and (in my conscyence) agaynst
lawe of god z hys chyrche / whiche passeth all the reste / but
you among you have forgotten the kyng my father / yet both
gods comandment z nature wyll not suffre me to do so / where
with gods helpe J wyll remayne an obedyent chylde to hys law
as he lefte theym / tyll suche tyme as the kynge ma.te my broth
shall have parfayt yers of dyscrecyon to ordre the power that god
sent hym z to be a Jurde in theyse matters hym self / and J doubt
but he shall then accept my so doyng as well better then theyre
have taken a pece of his power vpon theym in his mynoryte

J do not a litle mervayle / that you can fynde faute wt me for obserua
of that lawe / whiche was allowed by hym that was a kyng not on
of power but also of knowledge howe to ordre hys power / to
and ymed at that tyme to the
apparance very well to lyke the same / and that you can fynde
faute is some amongste your selfes / for runnyng halfe a yere
that wt you call a law and before the byshopps cam together
me thynketh you do me very myche wrong if J shuld not have as
contyneu in kepyng a full authoryssd lawe
wtout partyalyte / as they had, lothe to breake the lawe wt at that
your selfes muste neds confesse was of full power z strengthe
vse alteracyons of theyr owne Jnvencyon contrarie both to that
to your nowe lawe as you call it

Mary's Mass

Autograph draft letter, unsigned, by Lady Mary, to the Lords of the Privy
Council, remonstrating with them for breaking the oaths they had sworn
to her late father, King Henry VIII, by introducing reformist religious
legislation. *c.* 1551.

British Library, Lansdowne MS 1236, f. 28

*It is no small grief to me to perceive that they whom the King's Majesty, my father
(whose soul God pardon) made in this world of nothing in respect of that they be come
to now, and at his last end put in trust to see his will performed, whereunto they were all
sworn upon a book. It grieveth me I say, for the love I bear to them, to see both how they
break his will, and what usurped power they take upon them, in making (as they call it)
laws both clean contrary to his proceedings and will, and also against the custom of all
Christendom, and (in my conscience) against the law of God and his Church, which
passeth all the rest. But though you, among you, have forgotten the King my father, yet
both God's commandment and nature will not suffer me to do so; wherefore with God's
help I will remain an obedient child to his laws as he left them 'til such time as the King's
Majesty my brother shall have perfect years of discretion to order the power that God
hath sent him, and to be a judge in these matters himself; and I doubt not but he shall then
accept my so doing better than theirs which have taken a piece of his power upon them in
his minority.*

 *I do not a little marvel that you can find fault with me for observing of that law which
was allowed by him that was a king not only of power, but also of knowledge how to
order his power, to which law all you consented, and seemed at that time to the outward
appearance very well to like the same; and that you can find no fault all this while with
some amongst yourselves, for running half a year before that which you now call a law, ye
and before the bishops came together, wherein me thinketh you do me very much wrong if
I should not have as much pre-eminence to continue in keeping a full authorized law made
without partiality, as they had, both to break the law which at that time yourselves must
needs confess was of full power and strength, and to use alterations of their own invention
contrary both to that ye and to your new law as you call it.*

As Lord President of the Council, Warwick had two main tasks: the first was to address the Crown's desperate financial situation and the second was to accelerate religious change. To prevent further drain on the treasury, Warwick quickly abandoned Somerset's costly war in Scotland and concluded peace with France by surrendering English-occupied Boulogne in return for a ransom. Crown lands were sold to raise revenue and royal debts called in. The disastrous policy of debasement introduced by Henry VIII in the 1540s was halted and steps were taken to revalue the debased coinage.

Encouraged by Edward VI's evangelical zeal and aided by Archbishop Thomas Cranmer, Warwick continued to advance the Protestant Reformation in England. In February 1550, Cranmer introduced a new Protestant *Ordinal* (an order of service for the ordination of bishops and priests) to replace the Catholic *Pontificale*. The *Ordinal* emphasized the importance of the clergy's role as preachers of the Word of God. It also sought to reduce ritual and ceremony in Church practice. Conservative bishops who refused to accept the new *Ordinal* were ousted from office and replaced with radical individuals, many of whom were Cranmer's protégés. Cranmer's young chaplain Nicholas Ridley replaced Edmund Bonner as Bishop of London and John Hooper returned from exile to become Bishop of Gloucester. The conservatives Nicholas Heath, Stephen Gardiner, George Day and Cuthbert Tunstall were deprived of their sees of Worcester, Winchester, Chichester and Durham, respectively.

The stripping of churches continued unabated, and elaborately decorated interiors became bare places of worship. Stone altars, symbolizing sacrifice and therefore implying transubstantiation, were ripped out and replaced with wooden Communion tables; religious statues, icons and paintings were destroyed and thousands of Latin prayer and service books were burned.

The high point of the Edwardian Reformation was the publication of the second *Prayer Book* of 1552, which was far more radical than the 1549 version and unambiguously Protestant. The most important change was to the nature of the Eucharist or 'Mass', which was henceforth to be called 'the Lord's Supper or Holy Communion'. Communion would now be celebrated not at an altar in an area of the east end of the church, reserved for clergy alone, but at the 'Lord's table' in the church nave. Most importantly, the doctrine of the Real

Presence of Christ in the Eucharist was repudiated: congregations would no longer be offered 'the Body of our Lord Jesus Christ', but instead be invited to 'take and eat this in remembrance that Christ died for thee and feed on him in thy heart with thanksgiving'. In April 1552, the new *Prayer Book* was authorized in a new Act of Uniformity, which also required every person living in England and Wales to attend church on Sundays. The following year, the English Church adopted Cranmer's Forty-Two Articles of Religion. As with the 1552 Prayer Book, the Articles were a clear statement of Reformed Protestant faith: the doctrine of justification by faith alone was firmly asserted and transubstantiation and 'sacrifice of Masses' denied.

Refusing to accept the legality of the reformist religious legislation, Edward's devoutly Catholic half-sister Mary wrote this indignant letter to the Lords of the Privy Council around 1551. She remonstrated with them for breaking the oaths they had sworn to her late father, King Henry VIII, and for ignoring his will 'in making … laws both clean contrary to his proceedings and will, and also against the custom of all Christendom, and (in my conscience) against the law of God and his Church'. Believing that Edward would reverse the religious reforms once he came of age, she continued 'I will remain an obedient child to his laws as he left them 'til such time as the King's Majesty my brother shall have perfect years of discretion to order the power that God hath sent him, and to be a judge in these matters himself.' Showing the same spirit and steely resolve as her late mother, Katherine of Aragon, Mary refused to conform to the 1549 Act of Uniformity and persisted in having Latin Mass celebrated in her household. In doing so, she misjudged her brother, who by 1551 would no longer tolerate her disobedience. On 28 January, the thirteen-year-old king informed his sister: 'It is a scandalous thing that so high a personage should deny our sovereignty.' Two months later, they met in an emotional showdown at Westminster, but neither Mary's tears nor her declaration that she was prepared to die for her faith persuaded Edward to back down. Even when Mary's pious cousin, the Holy Roman Emperor Charles V, intervened and threatened war if she was not allowed Mass, Edward remained as uncompromising as ever. For the next two years, the King maintained the ban on the Mass in Mary's private chapels.

Like as a shipman in stormy wether plukes downe the sailes tarijnge
for bettar winde, so did I, most noble Kinge, in my vnfortune
chanche a thursday pluk{ed} downe the hie sailes of my ioy and cofort
and do trust one day that as troblesome waues haue repuls{ed}
me bakwarde, so a gentil winde wil bringe me forwarde to
my hauen. Two chief occasions moued me muche and
grieued me gretly, the one for that I douted your Maiesti{es}
helthe, the other bicause for al my longe tarijnge I wente
withont that I came for, of the first I am releued in
a parte, bothe that I vnderstode of your helthe and also
that your Maiesties logmge is far fro my Lorde Marque{s}
chamber, Of my other grief I am not eased, but the best
is that whatsoeuer other folkes wil suspect, I intende not
to feare your graces goodwil, wiche as I knowe that
I neuer disarued to faint, so I trust wil stil stike by me
For if your graces admis that I shulde retourne (who{s}
wil is a comandemente) had not bime, I wold not haue
made the halfe of my way, the ende of my iourney.
And thus as one desirous to hire of your Maiesties helth
thogh vnfortunat to se it I shal pray God for euer to
preserue you. From Hatfilde this present saterday.

Your Maiesties humble sist{er}
to comandemente. Elizabeth

Death of Edward VI

Autograph letter by Princess Elizabeth, to her dying brother, King Edward VI, expressing her disappointment that she had been unable to visit him. Hatfield House, Spring 1553.

British Library, Harley MS 6986, f. 23

Like as a shipman in stormy weather plucks down the sails tarrying for better wind, so did I, most noble King, in my unfortunate chance a Thursday pluck down the high sails of my joy and comfort and do trust one day that as troublesome waves have repulsed me backward, so a gentle wind will bring me forward to my haven. Two chief occasions moved me much and grieved me greatly, the one for that I doubted your Majesty's health, the other because for all my long tarrying I went without that I came for. Of the first I am relieved in a part, both that I understood of your health, and also that your Majesty's lodging is [not] far from my Lord Marquis [of Northampton]'s chamber. Of my other grief I am not eased, but the best is that whatsoever other folks will suspect, I intend not to fear your Grace's goodwill, which as I know that I never deserved to faint, so I trust will still stick by me. For if your Grace's advice that I should return (whose will is a commandment) had not been, I would not have made the half of my way, the end of my journey. And thus as one desirous to hear of your Majesty's health, though unfortunate to see it, I shall pray God for ever to preserve you. From Hatfield this present Saturday.

Your Majesty's humble sister
to commandment Elizabeth.

The reign of Edward VI was ultimately to be one of unfulfilled potential, for, as the young King approached his sixteenth birthday and prepared to cross the threshold of power, he fell ill and died prematurely. The humanist Sir Richard Morrison lamented 'What a King should England have had if God had given him his father's age', and indeed the evidence does suggest that Edward possessed the intellectual ability and talent to become one of England's great rulers, had he survived to adulthood. As Lord President of the Privy Council, Warwick had tasked his private secretary, William Cecil, and the Secretary of State, Sir William Petre, with preparing the King for the business of government. From 1551, Edward was encouraged to attend the Privy Council, and his *Chronicle* and surviving policy papers, composed on subjects such as finance, trade, the reform of abuses in the Church and state and diplomacy, reveal that Edward had started to take a keen interest in the business of government and policy-making and had a well-developed understanding of the tasks that needed to be accomplished.

In the summer of 1552, Warwick, now Duke of Northumberland, decided that Edward was ready to go on his first royal progress to the southern counties of Sussex, Surrey, Hampshire and Dorset. Earlier that year, however, Edward recorded in his *Chronicle* that he had fallen ill with measles and smallpox. Although he seemed to make a full recovery, it is likely that his immune system was compromised, and he fell ill again sometime between returning to London in September and November, when his *Chronicle* comes to an abrupt end. The following spring, Princess Elizabeth was deeply concerned about Edward and set out from Hatfield House in Hertfordshire to visit him, only to be turned back mid-journey owing to his ill health. Back at Hatfield, she penned this letter, one of the last that she would send to her brother. Written in her elegant, humanistic italic hand, the letter is beautifully composed and showcases the future queen's masterful use of language, as well as her fondness for expressing herself metaphorically. In this case, Elizabeth used the image of a boat tossed on stormy seas to convey her disappointment at being prevented from visiting her brother. Her distress is understandable, for she and Edward were close in age and shared a genuine affection for each other, having spent much of their childhood together. Elizabeth assured Edward that she would ignore the circulating rumours that she was no longer in his favour, and instead trust that 'your Grace's goodwill ... will still stick by me'. She ended her letter by expressing her desire for news of Edward's health and with a promise that she would pray for his recovery.

By May 1553 it was clear to those surrounding the King that his illness, most likely acute pulmonary tuberculosis, was terminal. It was probably at this point that Edward and Northumberland decided to change the line of succession established by Henry VIII in the 1543 Act of Succession and confirmed in his last will and testament. The Act declared that if Edward died without heirs he was to be succeeded by Henry's eldest daughter Mary and that, if she also died childless, his youngest daughter Elizabeth should succeed her. Despite restoring both his daughters to the succession, Henry never removed the taint of illegitimacy from them and it was on the basis of their being of 'half-blood' that Edward justified excluding his half-sisters from the succession. Edward may well have believed their 'illegitimacy' made them unfit to succeed, but his primary reason for altering the succession was to protect the Protestant Reformation. To do so he had to prevent his resolutely Roman Catholic half-sister Mary from succeeding him.

Edward's 'Device for the Succession' survives today in the Inner Temple Library. Written in the King's own hand, it provided for the crown to pass directly to the Protestant male descendants of Henry VIII's younger sister Mary Tudor. Like his father before him, Edward had decided to bar the Scottish Catholic descendants of Henry VIII's elder sister Margaret from the succession. Problematically, however, neither Mary's daughter Frances, Duchess of Suffolk, nor her eldest daughter, Lady Jane Grey, had borne any sons. As it became clear that time was running out for Edward, he altered the wording of the 'Device', changing 'Lady Jane's heirs male' to 'Lady Jane and her heirs male' in order to bequeath the crown to his Protestant cousin, Lady Jane Grey, who had recently married the Duke of Northumberland's youngest son, Guildford Dudley. Edward VI died at the age of fifteen at Greenwich Palace on 6 July 1553, leaving behind him a contested royal succession, the consequences of which would be played out over the next thirteen days.

VERITAS ...TEMPORIS FIL...

QUEEN MARY. I.

Antonio Mc...

HONI SOIT QVI MAL Y PENSE

MARY I

Jane the Quene

Right trusty and welbiloved we grete yow well...
advertysing yow that wheras It hath pleased
almighty god to call to his mercye out of this
lyef our derest Cosyn the king your late
Sovereigne lorde by whose decease and such
ordinance as the sayd late king dyd establysh
in his lyef tyme for the suretie and welth
of this Realme we ar entred into our right...
... of this kyngdome and by the last
will of our sayd derest cosyn & lettres
patentes and other severall Instrumentes to
... signed with his owne hand and sealed
... the greate seale of this Realme in his...
owne presence whereunto the Nobles of this
Realme for the most parte and all our Counsaill
and Iustices with the Mayor and Aldermen
of our citie of London and dyverse other...
grave personages of this our Realme of England
have also subscribed their names as by the
same will and instrument it maye more...
evydently and playnely appere We therfore
doo yow tunderstande that by thordenance...
Inheritance of the Imperiall Crow and by the...
assent and consent of our sayd Nobles and
Counsaillo(u)rs and other aftr sperified we...
this daye make our entree into our Towre
of London as our right full Queene of the...
... Iustice... requyre yow herby...
to all our army subiectes lyveing they herby
tunderstande their dewtes of allegeaunce to...
they nowe owe but be ye not more imployed to...
the same we shall paynes preston and welbiloved...
nothing doubting right trusty and welbiloved...
but that ye will endevor yo(ur)self in all
thing to th'uttermost of yo(ur) powers not onely

to defende of iustie title but will assyst vs in owr
rightfull possessyon of this liberdom and to distourbe
repell and resyst the pretended and vntrewe
clayme of the Lady Marye bastard daughter
to owr dreade vncle Henry theight of famous
memorye wherinas ye shall doo that to vs
to yor honor great and dutie apptayneth
So shall we remembre the same vnto yow and
yors accordingly. And so further pleasse it that
ye shall contynue doo and execute every
thing and thinge vs os lieutenant within all
place according to the lawes of this reaulme
established but yor sonn os late contynynge
Edward the sixte in suche and lyke sorte vt
if the same had liued here we mynd shortly
it shalbe renneally and by yow confirmed given
owr dreade seale vnto yow ye & vnder owr
Sygnet at owr Towne of London the xxxx vijth
the first yere of owr reign

Queen Jane and Queen Mary

Letter signed by Lady Jane Grey, as Queen, to William Parr, Marquis
of Northampton, Lord Lieutenant of Surrey, Northampton, Bedford and
Berkshire, requesting his allegiance against the 'feigned and untrue claim of
the Lady Mary'. Tower of London, 10 July 1553.

British Library, Lansdowne MS 1236, f. 24r–v.

Jane the Queen

*Right trusty and well beloved cousin, we greet you well, advertising you that where it
hath pleased Almighty God to call to his mercy out of this life our dearest cousin the
King your late sovereign lord, by reason whereof and such ordinances as the said late King
did establish in his lifetime for the security and wealth of this realm, we are entered into
our rightful possession of this kingdom, as by the last will of our said dearest cousin, our
late progenitor, and other several instruments to that effect signed with his own hand and
sealed with the great seal of this realm in his own presence, whereunto the nobles of this
realm for the most part and all our Council and judges, with the mayor and aldermen of
our city of London, and divers other grave personages of this our realm of England, have
also subscribed their names, as by the same will and instrument it may more evidently and
plainly appear. We therefore do you to understand, that by the ordinance and sufferance
of the heavenly Lord and by the assent and consent of our said nobles and councillors,
and others before specified, we do this day make our entry into our Tower of London as
rightful Queen of this realm, and have accordingly set forth our proclamations to all our
loving subjects giving them thereby to understand their duty of allegiance which they now
owe unto us as more amply by the same you shall briefly perceive and understand. Nothing
doubting, right trusty and right well beloved, but that you will endeavour yourself in all
things to the uttermost of your power, not only to defend our just title, but also assist us
in our rightful possession of this kingdom, and to disturb, repel, and resist the feigned and
untrue claim of the Lady Mary bastard daughter to our great uncle Henry the Eight
of famous memory; wherein as you shall do that which to your honour, truth and duty
appertaineth, so shall we remember the same unto you and yours accordingly. And our
further pleasure is that ye shall continue, do and execute everything and things as our*

Lieutenant within all places, according to the tenor of the commission addressed unto you from our late cousin King Edward the Sixth in such and like sort as if the same had been, as we mind shortly it shall be, renewed, and by us confirmed under our great seal unto you.

Given under our signet at our Tower of London the xth of July, the first year of our reign.

E dward VI's death was initially kept secret while preparations were made for the accession of the sixteen-year-old Lady Jane Grey. On 10 July, accompanied by her new husband Guildford Dudley, Jane travelled by barge to the Tower of London, where she was greeted by John Dudley, Duke of Northumberland, and his fellow councillors and proclaimed Queen. Northumberland must have felt hugely relieved that Jane's accession had gone smoothly; he certainly had no reason to suspect that the plans he had put in place would unravel so quickly, for he had secured London and had control of the Tower of London, the Armoury, the Treasury and the Navy. However, his failure to capture Lady Mary before proclaiming Jane Queen was a serious error. Northumberland had in fact attempted to imprison Mary by luring her from her house at Hunsdon in Hertfordshire to her dying brother's bedside in London. But Mary was warned about the trap and evaded capture by fleeing to the safety of Kenninghall in Norfolk, where, on 9 July, she proclaimed herself rightful Queen. Northumberland, like many others, had underestimated Mary who, having already spent much of her embattled life defending her claim to the throne, was now more determined than ever to fight for it.

Mary now moved to the more secure Framlingham Castle in Suffolk, where she raised her standard and started to muster forces. Mary was very popular with the provincial aristocracy and gentry and many – Protestant and Catholic alike – rallied to her side as the legitimate heir to the throne. Just days after Jane's coronation, the groundswell of popular support for Mary revealed the fragility of Jane's hold on the throne. Northumberland and Henry Grey, Duke of Suffolk instructed Jane to send circular letters to the Lieutenants of different counties to demand their allegiance against the 'feigned and untrue claim of the Lady Mary bastard daughter to our great uncle Henry the Eight'. This one, written by a secretary and signed by 'Jane the Queen' was sent to William Parr, Marquis of Northampton and brother of the late Queen, Katherine Parr, in his capacity as Lord Lieutenant of the counties of Surrey, Northampton, Bedford and Berkshire.

As Mary marched south towards London, accompanied by some 30,000 supporters, Northumberland raised troops and, on 14 July, set out from London to seize her. Meanwhile, news reached Jane's councillors back at the Tower that more of the country, including the Thames Valley, the Midlands and the West Country, had risen up in favour of Mary as Edward's rightful heir. Their mood grew increasingly defeatist and a large number of them, led by the Earls of Arundel, Shrewsbury, Bedford and Pembroke, deserted Jane and declared for Mary. On 19 July, thirteen days after the death of Edward, Mary was proclaimed Queen of England and London erupted into jubilant celebration. Jane's father, the Duke of Suffolk, broke the news to his daughter before proclaiming Mary Queen on Tower Hill. The following day, Northumberland, realizing that the plot to alter the succession had failed, surrendered and proclaimed Mary Queen in the market square at Cambridge. By the time Mary made her triumphal state entry into London on 3 August, he had been arrested and committed to the Tower, where he was executed on 22 August. Somewhat surprisingly, the Duke of Suffolk was pardoned without a trial, while Jane and Guildford were tried and convicted of high treason. The Queen believed that the couple were innocent of intent and granted a reprieve from the death sentence. It was expected that she would eventually pardon the couple, but for the time being they were left imprisoned in the Tower.

On 30 September, Mary's coronation procession passed through the City of London, giving Londoners the opportunity to see their new sovereign. The grand procession consisted of barons, nobles and gentlemen, knights, judges, bishops, members of the Privy Council, ambassadors and merchants. The Queen was immediately preceded by her personal entourage, which included the Earls of Arundel and Oxford and the eighty-year-old Thomas Howard, Duke of Norfolk, who, having been imprisoned by Henry VIII in 1547, had recently been released by the new Queen. Mary travelled in an open litter pulled by six horses and was 'richly apparelled with mantle and kirtle [gown] of cloth of gold' and wore a 'circlet of gold set with rich stones and pearls' on her head. In the next carriage were Mary's half-sister, the Princess Elizabeth, and Henry VIII's fourth wife, Anne of Cleves, followed by a large number of peeresses, gentlewomen and ladies-in-waiting. The next day, Mary was crowned Queen of England at Westminster Abbey. Against all the odds, she had won the throne to become England's first ruling queen, and, in doing so, succeeded in preserving the Tudor succession.

Marye, the quene:

The Quenes Highnes most excellent Ma.tie ponderyng how Sir Thomas Wyat confederat w other lewde & evill disposed psonnes haue vnder the ptense of the ben of the comen welth of the Realme to wthstande str herte sette furth in a proclamaxion, herby to assemble Highnes good true and lovinge subiects, to the disturbaunc of the realme, the confusion of this comen welth and destruaxion of her most noble psonne and astate (wherby pebill) her said Highnes beinge wisefully moved forward the consvaxion of her subiects from all pill and daunger glad to deliver suche as sholde be by sinistre motions w and seduced: Hathe thought good to signifie to her said sub that whosoever vpon eny proclamaxion made and sette by the said Thomas or eny other that man, to the pur aforesayde shall happen to assemble accordinge to same, and vpon knowlege herof shall w in xxiiij. howe after returne to their howses and like their quietly & obedintly: Her Highnes is contented to pdonne ther th comyng in the said assemblie, and to defend and mainte them as her Highnes good subiects to the benefit and comforte of them and their posterite.

Wyatt's Rebellion

Queen Mary's 'Proclamation of pardon to such of Sir Thomas Wyatt's followers as should, within twenty-four hours of the knowledge thereof, depart peaceably to their homes'. January 1554.

British Library, Cotton MS Vespasian F iii, f. 24

By the Queen

Mary the Queen

The Queens Highness most excellent Majesty, understanding how Thomas Wyatt, confederate with other lewd and evil disposed persons, have, under the pretence of the benefit of the commonwealth of the Realm, to withstand strangers, set forth a proclamation thereby to assemble her Highness' good, true and loving subjects, to the disturbance of the realm, the confusion of this commonwealth, and the destruction of her most noble person and estate (which God forbids), her said Highness being mercifully moved towards the conservation of her subjects from all peril and danger, and glad to relieve such as should be by sinister motions abused and seduced: hath thought good to signify to her said subjects, that whosoever, upon any proclamation made and set forth by the said Thomas, or any other private man, to the purpose aforesaid, shall happen to assemble according to the same, and upon knowledge hereof, shall within xxiiii hours after, return to their houses and live there quietly and obediently: her Highness is contented to pardon that their doing in the said assembly, and to defend and maintain them as her Highness's good subjects, to the benefit and comfort of them and their posterity.

[Issued under the Queen's signet and sign manual]

As Queen, Mary had a duty to marry and produce an heir. Already thirty-seven years old, she resolved to find a husband as quickly as possible and sought guidance on the matter from her cousin, Emperor Charles V. On 27 October 1553, Mary informed her Privy Council that she intended to marry Charles' son and heir, Prince Philip of Spain. Although the proposed union would revive the Anglo–Spanish alliance and was therefore politically expedient, it proved extremely unpopular with Mary's subjects, who disliked the idea of a Catholic foreigner sharing the English throne. On 16 November, Parliament petitioned Mary to take an English husband instead, but she refused to allow Parliament to dictate whom she should marry. Charles V's ambassadors arrived in early January 1554 to negotiate the marriage treaty, the terms of which were publicized two weeks later: Philip would be titled 'King of England' during Mary's lifetime but not hold any regal powers. He was, however, to assist the Queen in the administration of her realm. He could not embroil England in Habsburg wars nor appoint any 'aliens' to English office. Mary and Philip's heirs would inherit the throne of England and the Netherlands, while Philip's son from his first marriage would inherit Spain and the Habsburg lands in Italy. If the marriage failed to produce any heirs, Philip would have no right of succession.

Although the treaty preserved Mary's legal rights as Queen and limited Philip's powers as King Consort, public discontent remained strong. Four Protestant aristocrats, including Lady Jane Grey's father, the Duke of Suffolk, plotted simultaneous uprisings in Kent, Hereford, Leicester and Devon, which would converge on London, depose Mary and replace her with the Protestant Princess Elizabeth. The insurrections were planned to take place at the end of March but, when plans leaked out in January, the conspirators were forced to act sooner than anticipated and only the Kent rebellion got off the ground. Sir Thomas Wyatt, courtier and son of the famous poet Thomas Wyatt, managed to raise an army of some 3,000 rebels and marched on the capital from Kent. The situation looked increasingly alarming when a force of London militia, being led by the elderly Duke of Norfolk to confront Wyatt at Rochester, joined the rebels. With Wyatt and his supporters fast approaching, Mary's Council tried to negotiate and Mary issued an official proclamation of pardon, shown here, to all those who returned to their houses within twenty-four hours to live 'quietly and obediently'. Interestingly, due to the large number of proclamations that needed to be issued and with extreme haste, they were signed using the wet stamp of the Queen's sign manual (signature) and not by Mary herself. The negotiations failed and, on 31 January, Wyatt and his men were declared traitors. Mary refused to flee to the safety of Windsor Castle, opting instead to remain in London to rally support. On 1 February, the Queen made a rousing speech at the Guildhall, denouncing Wyatt, defending her choice of husband and calling on Londoners to stand firm against the rebels. Wyatt had expected London to support him but instead found the city gates shut against him. With his supporters fading away, Wyatt was forced to surrender to the Queen's forces and he was executed on 11 April for high treason.

The failure of Wyatt's rebellion sealed the fate of Lady Jane Grey and her husband Guildford Dudley, who had remained in the Tower of London since their arrest the previous year for high treason. Although they themselves were innocent of any involvement in Wyatt's conspiracy, the Duke of Suffolk's leadership of the uprising in Leicestershire undermined Mary's belief that the Greys had been victims of the Duke of Northumberland's ambition. Moreover, the Queen's advisers warned her that Jane would inevitably become the figurehead of future Protestant plots, thus making her dangerous. Mary sent John Feckenham, her own confessor and Dean of St Paul's, to the Tower in the hope that he would be able to convert Jane to the Catholic faith, but she remained steadfast in her Protestant belief until the end. On 12 February, Lady Jane Grey and her husband Guildford Dudley were executed.

Princess Elizabeth was also suspected of complicity in Wyatt's rebellion, although no actual evidence existed to support this charge. On 16 March she was committed to the Tower, where she was interrogated by the Queen's ministers. Elizabeth protested her innocence and Wyatt cleared her name moments before he was executed on Tower Hill. Elizabeth was released on 19 May – exactly eighteen years to the day since her mother, Anne Boleyn, had been executed in the Tower – but she remained a potential threat to Mary's regime and was therefore placed under house arrest at Woodstock Palace in Oxfordshire until April 1555.

Instructions for my lorde previséll

fyrste to tell the kyng the whole state of this reali
wt all thyngs apparteynyng to the same asmuche as
knowe to be trewe

seconde to obey hys comandment in all thyngs

thyrdly in all thyngs he shall aske your aduyse, to
your opinion as becometh a faythfull conceyllour to

Marye the quene

Reconciliation with Rome

Queen Mary's autograph instructions to the Lord Privy Seal concerning her new husband, Philip II of Spain. 1554.

British Library, Cotton MS Vespasian F iii, f. 23

Instructions for my Lord Privy Seal

First to tell the King the whole state of this Realm, with all things appertaining to the same, as much as you know to be true.

Second, to obey his commandment in all things.

Thirdly, in all things he shall ask your advice, to decl[are] your opinion as becometh a faithful councillor to do.

Mary the Queen.

The fierce opposition that Mary encountered made her even more determined to marry Philip. She would, she declared, 'wed no other man'. The thirty-eight-year-old Queen finally met her twenty-seven-year-old Spanish prince at Winchester just days before they were married in the Cathedral there on 25 July 1554. Mary's subjects had been assured that, according to the terms of the marriage treaty, Philip would be 'rather as a subject than otherwise; and that the Queen should rule all things as she doth now'. Shown here is a small piece of paper bearing Mary's handwritten instructions to Lord Russell, Keeper of the Privy Seal, who led an embassy to Spain to escort Philip back to England. Her instructions 'to tell the King the whole state of this Realm' and 'to obey his commandment in all things' suggest that Mary had a different view of the marriage and clearly intended for Philip to help her manage affairs of state.

Mary's steadfast allegiance to the Roman Catholic faith had undoubtedly influenced her decision to marry Philip and there were those who feared that her marriage would inevitably lead to the formal restoration of papal authority. Mary's greatest desire was certainly to restore Catholicism and return the English Church to pre-Reformation glory – the world of her childhood, which Henry VIII had destroyed when he broke with Rome in order to divorce her mother, Katherine of Aragon. As Queen, Mary believed that she had a divinely given opportunity to 'put things right', and she was determined to do so. Shortly after becoming Queen she issued a proclamation, declaring her inability 'to hide that religion which God and the world knoweth she hath ever professed from her infancy'. She urged her new subjects to follow her religion, but promised to force no one's conscience. When Mary's first Parliament convened on 5 October 1553, it repealed the Act of Supremacy and, by the end of the year, Mary had ceased to use the title of Supreme Head of the Church. Edward VI's religious legislation was also overturned, making Mass legal again and restoring the rites and ceremonies of the last year of Henry VIII's reign.

The next stage of Mary's plan was to restore Catholicism as the state religion and to reunite England with Rome. In this, she was encouraged and assisted by Philip, who negotiated the return of Cardinal Reginald Pole to England as papal legate. Of royal blood himself, Pole had been favoured by Henry VIII as a young man but had fallen out with the King and forced into exile over plans to divorce Katherine of Aragon and break with Rome. Pole returned to England in November 1554, empowered by Pope Julius III to reconcile England with Rome. On 30 November, addressing Philip, Mary and Parliament, Pole explained that he had come to rebuild true religion, grant England absolution for its heresy and receive it back into the Catholic Church. From this point on, Mary's regime became more vengeful towards its Protestant enemies. The medieval heresy laws, which had been used against Protestants by Henry VIII before being repealed by Edward Seymour, Duke of Somerset, in 1547, were revived and, from February 1555 until the end of Mary's reign, nearly 300 Protestants were burned at the stake, earning the Queen the sobriquet 'Bloody Mary'. The first victim was John Rogers, who was burned on 4 February 1555 for preaching against 'pestilent popery and idolatry and superstition'. The most high-profile martyrs were Hugh Latimer, Bishop of Worcester, and Nicholas Ridley, Bishop of London, who died together in Oxford in October 1555, and Thomas Cranmer, former Archbishop of Canterbury, who went to the stake the following March. Cranmer bitterly regretted that he had renounced his Protestant beliefs following his arrest and on the day of his execution he publicly proclaimed the truth of the Protestant faith before famously thrusting the hand with which he had signed his recantations into the flames first.

After thirteen months of marriage to Mary, Philip left England to succeed his father Charles V as King Philip II of Spain. Philip only returned to England once more, in March 1557, to persuade Mary to support Spain in a renewed war against France, which resulted in the humiliating loss of Calais, England's last territorial possession on the continent. The failure of Philip and Mary's marriage to produce children dealt a painful blow to Mary's dream of a Catholic, Tudor heir to ensure the long-term restoration of Catholicism in England. It was only as she lay dying that Mary acknowledged that, in accordance with Henry VIII's will, her half-sister Elizabeth would be her successor to the throne – painfully aware that Elizabeth would establish a new Protestant order. Mary I died in St James's Palace on 17 November 1558, followed just hours later by Cardinal Pole.

VERA EFFIGIES REGINÆ ETc. ... PERENNIS ... SERENISSIMÆ PRINCIPIS ELIZABETHÆ ANGLIÆ FRANCIÆ ET HIBE.

Hauinge reformed Religion, established Peace, reduced Coyne to y^e iuste
value, Deliuered Scotland from ye Frenche, Reuenged domesticall Rebe:
saued Fraunce from headlonge ruyne by ciuell Warr supported Belleia,
ouerthrowe ye Spanishe inuincible Nauie, expelled ye Spaniard out of
Irelande, and receaued the Irishe into mercie, enriched England by

ELIZABETH I

It maye please youre grace to understand that
Albeyt the longe contynuance and vehemencye of my sycknes
besurye, as justely myght move me, rashynge awaye all the
cares of this worlde, onely to thyncke of that to come: yet
not beynge convenyent for me to determyne of lyefe or
death, whyche ys onely in the hande of god, I thought
yt my dutye, before I shuld departe, so myche as I coulde
to leave all persons satysfyed of me, and especyally your
grace, beynge of that honor and dygnytye, that the
provydence of god hathe called yo' unto. for which
purpose I do send yo' at this present myne almoner
faythfull Chapleyn the Deane of worcester, to which
yt maye please yo' grace to gyve credyte in that
shall saye unto yo' of my behalfe. I nothynge do
but that yo' grace shall remayne satysfyed therby
whom Almyghtye god longe prospere to hys honor
yo' comfort and wealthe of the Realme. From
Lambehyth the xxiijth daye of November. 15...

By yo' grace Orato'

Reg Car Cantuarie

Elizabeth I's Religious Settlement, 1559

Letter dictated and signed by Reginald, Cardinal Pole, Archbishop of
Canterbury, to Princess Elizabeth. Lambeth Palace, 14 November 1558.

British Library, Cotton MS Vespasian F iii, f. 28

*It may please your Grace to understand that albeit the long continuance and vehemence
of my sickness be such, as justly might move me, casting away all the cares of this world,
only to think of that to come. Yet not being convenient for me to determine of life or death,
which is only in the hand of God, I thought it my duty, before I should depart, so nigh
as I could to leave all persons satisfied of me, and especially your Grace, being of that
honour and dignity, that the providence of God hath called you unto. For which purpose
I do send you at this present mine ancient faithful Chaplain the Dean of Worcester, to
whom it may please your Grace to give credit in that he shall say unto you of my behalf.
I nothing doubt but that your Grace shall remain satisfied thereby, whom Almighty God
long prosper to his honour, your comfort and wealth of the realm. From Lambeth, the xiiii
day of November 1558.*

By your Grace's Orator,
Reginald, Cardinal, Archbishop of Canterbury.

Elizabeth's accession to the throne on 17 November 1558 ended a terrible period of personal insecurity and uncertainty in her life. Yet, as Queen, she would face a different set of challenges. In 1558, the most pressing of these was which religion she would establish in her realm. This letter was delivered to Elizabeth by Seth Holland, Cardinal Pole's chaplain, three days before she ascended the throne. There can be little doubt that the dying Archbishop's private message, conveyed to the queen-in-waiting by Holland, exhorted her to maintain the Catholic faith in England. However, Pole's request was futile, for although Elizabeth had outwardly conformed to Catholicism and accepted the Mass during Mary's reign, she was inclined to the Protestant faith and believed it was her duty to restore 'the true godly religion' to England.

Elizabeth was at Hatfield House when she first learned of Mary's death. The new Queen quickly gathered a group of advisers around her, and, most importantly, appointed Sir William Cecil, who had served in government under Edward VI and was a committed Protestant, as her principal secretary. For the next forty years, he would dedicate himself to serving the Queen and the Protestant cause.

In the early months of Elizabeth's reign it was widely anticipated that she would repudiate papal authority, but, beyond that, her religious intentions remained unclear. Unlike Mary, Elizabeth did not make any immediate announcements, but her actions gradually revealed her religious leanings. On Christmas Day, Elizabeth walked out of the Chapel Royal during the Mass when the consecrated elements were elevated, and days later she issued a proclamation that permitted her subjects to hear the litany, the Lord's Prayer and the Creed in English. At Elizabeth's coronation service in Westminster Abbey, the Epistle and the Gospel were read in English as well as Latin, but, most revealing of all, as the Mass was celebrated she slipped behind a screen to take Communion in both kinds (bread and wine).

Behind the scenes, Elizabeth and her ministers tackled the complex issue of shaping the religious settlement. The Queen urged tolerance and moderation and sought a broad, inclusive settlement to unite as many of her subjects as possible. The 'Device for the Alteration of Religion', a policy document probably produced by Cecil, set out a plan to make Protestantism the established religion of England. It urged that the alteration be attempted 'at the next Parliament ... for the sooner that religion is restored, God is the more glorified, and as we trust will be more merciful unto us, and better save and defend Her Highness from all dangers.'

Two pieces of religious legislation were introduced at Elizabeth's first Parliament, which convened on 25 January 1559: the (second) Act of Supremacy, which re-established the Church of England's independence from Rome and recognized Elizabeth as Supreme Governor of her Church and the (third) Act of Uniformity, which enforced the use of Cranmer's 1552 *Prayer Book* with some modifications to the wording of the Communion service to imply the Real Presence of Christ in the sacrament, thereby making it more acceptable to Elizabeth's Catholic subjects. It also allowed for continuity in some Catholic practices such as liturgy and vestments to please those subjects – and Elizabeth – who remained attached to the old ways.

The bills faced stiff opposition in the House of Lords, particularly from Mary's bishops, but they were eventually passed on 29 April 1559 and received the Queen's approval on 8 May. Elizabeth's religious settlement proved unacceptable to both Catholics loyal to Rome, and radical Protestants, who demanded further reform. Although Elizabeth did not want to tell her subjects what to believe – she is famously supposed to have said she had no 'liking to make windows into men's hearts and secret thoughts' – she nevertheless expected their loyalty and obedience to her religious laws. All subjects, therefore, had to attend church at least once a week or be fined. Catholic bishops who refused to take the Oath of Supremacy were imprisoned and replaced by new Protestant bishops, and as many as 2,000 parish clergy who refused to endorse the new settlement lost their parishes.

Elizabeth and Cecil's religious legislation of 1559 was nevertheless a remarkable achievement and turned England into a strong Protestant state without religious persecution or civil war. Despite the fact that in 1559 many hoped for further reformation, there would be no more changes to the Church of England's structures or practices during Elizabeth's reign. In 1563, the Thirty-Nine Articles of Religion were written under the guidance of Matthew Parker, Elizabeth's first Archbishop of Canterbury. The Articles provided the doctrinal foundation of the English Church and established, together with the Elizabethan *Book of Common Prayer*, the theology and form of worship that, in essence, still exists in the Church of England today.

With a sorrowfull harte, aud watery eies, J your poore snant and most
lowlye subiect, an vnworthy secretory, besech your Ma.ty: to pardon this
my lowlye suite. That considring the proceding in this matter for
removing of y.e french owt of Scotland, doth not content your Ma.ty,
and that J can not w. my conscience gyve any contrary advise, y.t J
may be w. your Ma.t favor, and clemency, be spared to entermeddle
therin, and this J am forced to doo of nesesite. for J will never be a
minister in any your Ma.t servire, wherunto your owne mynd shall not
be agreable. for thereunto J am sworne, to be a minister of your
Ma.t cÕmynations and not of myne owne, or of others though they be
never so many. and on the other part to serve yo.r Ma.t in any
thyng y.t my self can not allow, must nedes be an vnprofitable
service, and so vntoward, as therin J wold be loth your Ma.th shuld
be deceyved. and as for any other price, though it wer in your Ma.t
kytchen or garden from y.e bottom of my harte J am redy went
respect of estymable welth, or ease, to doo your Ma.t cÕmandmet
to my lyves end. wherof J wish w. all my poore sorrowfull hart y.t yo.r
Ma.t wold make some proofe. for this J doo affirme y.t J have not had
sence your Ma.t reigne, any one dayes ioye, but in your Ma.t honor, and welth:

Victory in Scotland

Autograph draft letter, unsigned, by William Cecil, to Elizabeth I, offering his resignation. ?December 1559.

British Library, Lansdowne MS 102, f. 1

It may please your most excellent Majesty
With a sorrowful heart and watery eyes, I your poor servant and most lowly subject, an unworthy secretary, beseech your Majesty to pardon this my lowly suit. That considering the proceeding in this matter for removing of the French out of Scotland doth not content your Majesty, and that I cannot with my conscience give any contrary advise, that I may be with your Majesty's favour and clemency, be spared to intermeddle therein. And this I am forced to do of necessity for I will never be a minister in any your Majesty's service, whereunto your own mind shall not be agreeable. For thereunto I am sworn to be a minister for your Majesty's determinations and not of mine own, or of others though they be never so many. And on the other part, to serve your Majesty in anything that myself cannot allow must needs be an unprofitable service and so untoward as therein I would be loath your Majesty should be deceived. And as for any other service, though it were in your Majesty's kitchen or garden, from the bottom of my heart I am ready without respect of estimation, wealth, or ease to do your Majesty's commandment to my life's end. Whereof I wish with all my poor, sorrowful heart that your Majesty would make some proof, for this I do affirm that I have not had since your Majesty's reign any one day's joy but in your Majesty's honour and weal.

In April 1559, Elizabeth I signed the Treaty of Cateau-Cambrésis, to extricate England from the disastrous war in France, which Philip II of Spain had persuaded Mary I to join. The peace agreement failed to reassure William Cecil, who was convinced that the great Catholic powers of France and Spain planned to destroy Protestant England and replace the 'heretical' Elizabeth with Mary, Queen of Scots, whom they believed to be Mary I's rightful heir. For not only was Mary a Catholic through her paternal line, she was also the great-granddaughter of Henry VII of England. Moreover, Mary was married to Francis, *dauphin* of France, and their union had strengthened the bond between France and Scotland, England's traditional enemies.

French influence in Scotland had been dangerously strong for a number of years, but, since 1554, Mary's French mother, Marie of Guise, had governed Scotland in her daughter's absence, bringing French power uncomfortably close to England. Marie pursued a pro-French policy: appointing French advisers and stationing several thousand French troops in Scotland. Consequently, Cecil's great fear was a French invasion from across the border. In July 1559, the death of Henry II of France, following a jousting accident, placed Mary's husband on the throne as Francis II. With Mary now Queen of France as well as Scotland, the prospect of a French invasion of England greatly increased. Cecil was alarmed to hear reports that Mary and Francis were making public their claim to Elizabeth's throne by adopting the English royal arms as their own.

On 11 May 1559, three days after Elizabeth gave her royal assent to the new religious legislation in England, a Protestant revolution broke out in Scotland. It was sparked by an inflammatory sermon against Catholic 'idolatry' by the famous Scottish reformer John Knox, who had recently returned to Scotland from exile in Europe. The revolt was led by a group of disaffected Scottish Protestant nobility, who called themselves the Lords of the Congregation and plotted to overthrow Marie of Guise to rid Scotland of Catholicism and French domination. By October, the Scottish Lords had seized Edinburgh and deposed Marie but needed financial and military aid from England in order to sustain their victory. Seeing an opportunity to secure England's northern border, Cecil favoured supporting the Scottish rebels to encourage religious change and destroy French power in Scotland. Elizabeth, however, was opposed to supporting the Protestant rebels against their rightful sovereign. She disliked

John Knox and his radical Protestantism and was reluctant to spend money on military intervention. Sometime in November, Elizabeth informed Cecil of her decision and he threatened to resign. Shown here is Cecil's letter to the Queen, written in his instantly recognizable angular hand, and, apparently, 'with a sorrowful heart and watery eyes'. He was sure that Elizabeth's decision about Scotland was wrong and it would therefore be 'an unprofitable service' for him to serve her 'in anything that myself cannot allow'.

Cecil's letter had the desired effect and in February 1560 Elizabeth signed the Treaty of Berwick with the Scottish Lords, which confirmed the provision of English military aid. Nevertheless, it was with great reluctance that Elizabeth agreed to send English troops to support a military attack on Leith and only then after she had been warned by her Privy Council that a French invasion was imminent and Mary and Francis 'be in their hearts mortal enemies to your Majesty's person'. The Anglo–Scottish siege of Leith was not the outright military success that Cecil had hoped for but, fortunately, the French were ready to make peace owing to growing religious and political dissension within their realm and the death of Marie of Guise. Cecil personally handled the negotiations, which concluded with the signing of the Treaty of Edinburgh on 6 July. This was a personal triumph for Cecil and firmly established him as the Queen's chief minister. It was also a truly historic moment, for the treaty effectively ended the 'Auld Alliance' between France and Scotland and replaced it with an Anglo-Scottish alliance. Under the terms of the treaty, France recognized Elizabeth's right to the English throne and Mary and Francis were to abandon their use of the English royal arms. Mary and Francis refused to ratify the treaty but it made little difference. The French withdrew from Scotland and a council of Scottish nobles was formed to govern the country. It lost no time in pushing a Protestant Reformation through Parliament.

In December 1560, Francis II died and was succeeded by his brother Charles IX. Aged just eighteen, the dowager Queen Mary was left excluded from political power in France and had little choice but to return to Scotland, a move that would soon cause enormous problems for Elizabeth's government.

that promis the yssew not wel, fynd and began thes attempts
others that respected the necessary facts of the matters
and no most vnderstood circumstances expedient
not to haue byne forgotten therin, others
whos cares wer deluded by pleasing pswations of
comen good whan the very yelding to ther owne
inventions might haue bred all your woes
others whos capacities I suppose yelded ther iugement
to ther frindes wit oppn' other that serued an
ecchoes place wel amonge all this sondry
affects I assure you ther be none whom
I better estceme for well mynded to me
or do suspect not to be my most loyall
subiects therfor I conclud with this oppinion
wiche I wyll you to thinke vnfaynedly tru
that as I haue tried that you may be dcceavd
so am I pswaded you wel not begile the assured
ioy that euer I toke to be my subiects love to
me more staunche than euer I felt the care for my self
my self to be great wiche alone hath made
my heuy burden light and a kyngdome
care but easy carriage for me wiche if I hap not
more for seo'cuiue than for glory I could
wish my self wiche a wetbay and vsome
let this my disputing stand you in stede
of borow strokes neuer to tempt to far
a princes pacience and let my comfort
plucke vp nour dismaied sprite and auoyd
in hope that your folowing obediances shall make vp your
you tyme that you wer retorne with your
princes gracis. and whose care for
you dowbt you not to be suche as she
shall not nide a remembrancer for your
weale

All this letter was the Queene's owne hand and the draught she framed her selfe.

CART. COTT. IV. 38. (2)

Marriage and Succession

Autograph draft of Elizabeth I's speech dissolving Parliament, rebuking them for their unwelcome 'lip-laboured orations' on the matter of her marriage and succession. January 1567.

British Library, Cotton Ch. IV. 38 (2)

I love so evil counterfeiting and hate so much dissimilation that I may not suffer you depart without that my admonitions may show your harms and cause you shun unseen peril. Two visors have blinded the eyes of the lookers-on in this present session, so far forth as, under pretence of saving all, they have done none good. And these they be: the succession and liberties. As to the first, the prince's opinion and goodwill ought, in good order, have been felt in other sort than in so public a place be uttered. It had been convenient that so weighty a cause had had his original from a zealous prince's consideration, not from so lip-laboured orations out of such ~~jangling~~ subjects' mouths, which, what the[y] be, time may teach you know and their demerits will make them acknowledge how the[y] have done their lewd endeavour to make all my realm suppose that their care was much when mine was none at all. Their handling of this doth well show, they being wholly ignorant, how fit my grant at this time should be to such a demand. In this one thing their imperfect dealings are to be excused, for I think this be the first time that so weighty a cause passed from so simple men's mouths as began this cause.

As to liberties, who is so simple that doubts whether a prince that is head of all the body may not command the feet not to stray when they would slip? God forbid that your liberty should make my bondage, or that your lawful liberties should anyways have been infringed. No, no, my commandment tended no whit to that end, the lawfulness of which commandment, if I had not more pitied you than blamed you, might easily by good right be showed you, perchance to their shame that bred you that coloured doubt. You were sore seduced. You have met with a gentle prince, else your needless scruple might perchance have bred your caused blame. And albeit the soothing of such be reprovable in all, yet I would not you should think my simplicity such as I cannot make distinctions among you, as of some that broached the vessel not well fined, and began these attempts, not foreseeing well the end; others that respected the necessary fetches [end] of the matters and no whit understood circumstances expedient not to have been forgotten therein; others whose ears were deluded by pleasing persuasions of common good when the very yielding to their own inventions might have bred all your woes; others whose capacities, I suppose, yielded their judgement to their friends' wit; some other that served an echo's place.

Well among all these sundry effects, I assure you there be none, the beginners only except, whom I either condemn for evil-minded to me or do suspect not to be my most loyal subjects.

Therefore I conclude with this opinion, which I will you to think unfeignedly true: that as I have tried that you may be deceived, so am I persuaded you will not beguile the assured joy that ever I took to see my subjects' love to me more staunch than ever I felt that care in myself for myself to be great, which alone hath made my heavy burden light and a kingdom['s] care but easy carriage for me. Let this my displing [disciplining] stand you in stead of sorer strokes never to tempt too far a prince's patience, and let my comfort pluck up your dismayed sprites [spirits] and cause you think that, in hope that your following behaviours shall make amends for past actions, you return with your prince's grace: whose care for you, doubt you not, to be such as she shall not need a remembrancer for your weal.

1563 See fol. 92 A lettre in Queen Elizabeth hand to the Commons in Parlament
5to Eliz 94 a. about ther petition concerning marriage and Libertyes

I love so evil counterfetting and hate so muche dissimulation
that I may not suffer you depart without that
my admonitions may shewe your harmes and cause
you shun unseen peril. Two ~~clokes~~ visars have blinded the yes
of the lokers on in this present session, so farforthe
as under pretence of saving all thei have done none
good. And thes they be Succession and liberties. As
to the first the princes opinion and good wyl ought
in good order have bine felt in other sort than
in so publik a place ~~once to~~ to be uttered it had
bine convenient that so waighty a cause had had
his original from a zelous princes consideration not fro
so lippe labored orations out of suche ~~ramping~~ subiectz
mouthes which what thei be time may teache you
knowe and ther demerites wyl make them
acknowledge how thei have done ther lewde endevour
to make all my realme suppose that ther care
was muche when myne was none at all. Ther
handeling of this dothe shewe the being wholly ignorant
how fit my grant at this time shuld be to suche a demaund
In one thing ther imperfect dealings ~~are~~ be excused
for I think this be the first time that
so weighty a cause passed from so
simple mouthes as began this cause. As to liberties who is so simple that
doutis whither a prince that ~~is~~ is hed of all the
body may not comand the fete not to
stray when thei wold slip. God forbid that
your liberty shuld make my bondage or
or that your lawfull liberties shuld any wais have bine infringed
no no my comandement tended no whit to that end
the being not so ~~ther~~ you were sore seduced ~~and~~ you have met
with a gentil prince els your nidles scruple
perchance had bred your causeles blame
And albeit the sothing of suche be reprovable in all
yet I wold not you shuld thinke my simplicitie such
as I can not make distinctions amonge you as of some

A [illegible] of wysdoms [illegible] commandement [illegible] by good [illegible] pitied you that [illegible] you perchance to their shame that [illegible] that [illegible] lizabeth I's marriage was the other great issue to dominate the early years of her reign. Today we know that Elizabeth never married, but when she ascended the throne in 1558 no one would have predicted that Europe's most eligible female would remain single. Concerned that the future of the Tudor monarchy depended on the survival of one woman, Elizabeth's councillors regularly pressed her to marry and name an heir presumptive. In February 1559, Elizabeth responded graciously to the House of Commons' first formal petition and assured them that although she was not disposed towards marriage, she would not rule it out 'if it please God to incline my heart to another kind of life'. But she concluded with the prophetic words: 'In the end, this shall be for me sufficient, that a marble stone shall declare that a queen, having reigned such a time, lived and died a virgin.'

As a young queen, Elizabeth had many suitors to choose from and received marriage proposals from Philip II of Spain, the Archdukes Ferdinand and Charles of Austria and Eric XIV of Sweden. The Lords of the Congregation also proposed a marriage between Elizabeth and the Protestant James Hamilton, Earl of Arran, second in line to the Scottish throne, in order to strengthen ties with England. Elizabeth did not give serious consideration to any of her suitors, explaining that for the time being she wished to remain single. William Cecil was puzzled and frustrated by Elizabeth's reluctance to marry but, as Sir William Paget astutely commented to the Spanish ambassador in 1558, 'There is no one she can marry, outside the kingdom or within it.' Paget alone seems to have understood the dilemma that Elizabeth faced: if she married a foreign prince, she risked alienating her people, dragging England into foreign disputes, and jeopardizing the future independence of England. Alternatively, if she married one of her subjects, she feared it might create dangerous rivalries at court or trigger unrest in her realm.

The man Elizabeth came closest to marrying was the dashing and athletic Robert Dudley, her childhood friend and son of John Dudley, the Duke of Northumberland who had been executed for attempting to place Lady Jane Grey on the throne. As Queen, Elizabeth appointed Dudley Master of the Horse, a position which required him to accompany her whenever she rode out. By the spring of 1559, it was obvious that Elizabeth was in love with Dudley, who – despite being married – was soon suspected of being the reason why Elizabeth rebuffed other suitors. In September 1560, Dudley's wife died in mysterious circumstances. Eventually cleared of any involvement, Dudley sought to win the Queen's hand, but, after much agonizing, Elizabeth decided that she could not risk her reputation nor jeopardize her hold on power by marrying him.

In October 1562, Elizabeth's succession became a matter of even greater concern when she contracted smallpox. For a few days, the Queen's death looked imminent and Parliament feared a war of succession for the English throne between rival claimants Mary, Queen of Scots, and Lady Katherine Grey. As the granddaughter of Henry VIII's elder sister Margaret by her first marriage to James V of Scotland, Mary had the best hereditary claim, but was excluded from the English succession by Henry VIII's will. Furthermore, as a Catholic, Mary, Queen of Scots was an unacceptable candidate for many Protestants who favoured Catherine Grey, a descendant of Henry VIII's younger sister Mary and the rightful heir according to the terms of his 1543 Act of Succession, despite having a weaker hereditary claim. Elizabeth favoured the Scottish claim to the succession but steadfastly refused to recognize Mary as her heir; as she told the Scottish ambassador in 1561 it would be tantamount to 'setting my winding-sheet [shroud] before my eyes'. Elizabeth also knew from bitter personal experience that any named successor would soon become the focus of intrigue and conspiracy.

In November 1566, Parliament debated the Queen's succession again. Elizabeth was furious and tried unsuccessfully to silence the members on the subject. Shown here is the speech drafted by Elizabeth, in her atrocious cursive or 'business' hand, for the dissolution of Parliament the following January. The multiple scorings-out convey a sense of Elizabeth's rage as she severely rebukes them for their unwelcome 'lip-laboured orations' on the matter of her marriage and succession. She further berates her 'jangling subjects' (jangling is later crossed out) for exceeding the traditional liberties of Parliament by daring to express their views on so 'weighty a cause'. With regal hauteur, Elizabeth asks the members to consider 'who is so simple that doubts whether a prince that is head of all the body may not command the feet not to stray when they would slip?' Elizabeth concludes by warning them 'never to tempt too far a prince's patience'.

p_ 7tembre 1568

Mester knoleis y heuu hard sum neus from scotland y send
zou the douible off them y i reit to the quin my gud
sister and pres zou to du the lyk conforme to that
y spak zesternicht vnto zou and sut hest i ansur
y refer all to zour discretion and wil lipne beter
in zour gud delin for mi nor y kain persuad zou
nemli in this langasg excus my iuel vreitin for
y neuuer vsed it afor and am hestet ze schal
si my bel & huilk is opne it is sed se teraer
my vnfrinds wil bi vth zou y ser nething
bot trests weil and ze send oni to zour wiff
ze mey asur her schu wald a bin welcom to
a sur strenger hua nocht bien aquentet vth
her wil nocht bi ouuer beuld to vreit bot for
the aquentans betuix ous y wil send zou letle
tekne to rember zou off the gud hop y heuuin
zou guef ze send a mit mesager y wa lol
wysss ze bestouded it reder apon her non am
vder thus effter my commendations y prey god
heuuz u in hiskyin   Zour asured gud frind
                              Mari R

excus my iuel vreitin
Thus firist tym

The English Captivity of Mary, Queen of Scots

Autograph letter by Mary, Queen of Scots, to Sir Francis Knollys, asking him to intercede with Elizabeth I on her behalf. Bolton Castle, 1 September 1568.

British Library, Cotton MS Caligula C i, f. 218.

Master Knollys, I have heard some news from Scotland. I send you the double [copy] of them I wrote to the queen my good sister, and pray you to do the like, conform[able] to that I spoke [of] yesternight unto you, and send hasty answer. I refer all to your discretion, and will lissne [lean] better in your good dealing for me than I can persuade you, namely, in this language. Excuse my evil writing, for I never used it before and I am hasted. You shall see my bill [letter] which is open, it is said, Saturday my unfriends [enemies] will be with you. I say nothing, but trust well, and you send any[one] to your wife, you may assure her, she would a been welcome to a poor stranger, who, not being acquainted with her, will not be over-bold to write, but for the acquaintance between us I will send you a little token to remember you of the good hope I have in you. If ye find a meet messenger I would wish ye bestowed it rather upon her than any other. Thus after my commendations, I pray God have you in his keeping.

Your assured good friend
Mary R

Excuse my evil writing
this my first time.

Mary, Queen of Scots, left France on 14 August 1561 and arrived in Scotland twelve days later. The Scottish people were delighted to welcome their charming and beautiful Catholic queen home to her Protestant kingdom. Mary's rule began well, as she wisely agreed not to interfere in the nation's religious affairs and, in return, was allowed to practise Catholicism privately. She also appointed her Protestant half-brother Lord James Stuart as her principal adviser and quickly won the support of leading Protestant nobles.

Mary pursued a pro-English policy, frequently expressing her great desire for friendship with Elizabeth. The Scottish queen sent her English cousin friendly letters, small gifts and several requests for a personal meeting in the hope that she would eventually be officially recognized as Elizabeth's heir apparent. But Elizabeth resolutely refused to name her successor and caused further damage to relations with Mary by suggesting that she marry Robert Dudley, whom she had recently created the Earl of Leicester. While the proposed union made perfect sense to Elizabeth, who trusted Leicester to protect English interests against Scottish conspiracies, Mary was deeply affronted by the suggestion that she should marry the man widely believed to be Elizabeth's ex-lover. Unsurprisingly, Mary rejected Leicester and instead married her cousin Henry Stuart, Lord Darnley, the English-born grandson of Henry VIII's elder sister Margaret by her second husband Archibald, Earl of Angus. Elizabeth was furious, for, since Mary and Darnley were both great-grandchildren of Henry VII, their marriage strengthened Mary's claim to the English throne. The match was also unpopular in Scotland and it alienated many of the pro-English, Scottish Protestant politicians who had previously supported Mary, including James Stuart, now Earl of Moray.

Darnley was violent, arrogant and deeply unpopular, and, by the time Mary gave birth to their son, the future King James VI of Scotland and I of England, their marriage was effectively over. On the night of 9 February 1567, the house at Kirk o' Fields, in which Darnley was staying, just outside Edinburgh, was blown up. Darnley, whose body was later discovered in the garden, had been asphyxiated. His murder presented Mary, whose reign had been troubled for some time, with the opportunity to restore stability. She promptly squandered this opportunity by marrying James Hepburn, Earl of Bothwell, whom most people believed to be responsible for Darnley's murder.

Refusing to accept Bothwell as their king, nearly all the Scottish Lords rose against Mary. On 15 June 1567 she surrendered, was imprisoned in Lochleven Castle in Kinross-shire and forced to abdicate in favour of her infant son James, with the Earl of Moray appointed as regent. In May 1568, Mary escaped captivity and fled to England, naively expecting her cousin, Elizabeth I, to welcome her to court and to support her efforts to regain the Scottish throne. Mary's arrival created a huge dilemma for Elizabeth, who respected Mary as a fellow anointed sovereign, but was also aware of the threat she posed. For if Elizabeth invited Mary to court, her Catholic faith and claim to the English throne would make her an obvious focus for Catholic conspiracies. Similarly, if she provided military and financial support to restore Mary to her Scottish kingdom, she risked alienating the Protestant nobles who now governed Scotland.

While Elizabeth and her Council decided what to do about Mary, she was held first in Carlisle Castle and then in Bolton Castle under the close guard of Elizabeth's councillor and relative, Sir Francis Knollys. On 1 September 1568, Mary wrote this friendly letter to Knollys entreating him to intercede with Elizabeth on her behalf. It was the first letter that Mary, who had been raised in France, penned in English and at the foot of the letter she asks Knollys to 'Excuse my evil writing, this my first time'. William Cecil persuaded Elizabeth that it would be unwise to meet Mary or to release her. Instead, Elizabeth offered to mediate between Mary and the Scottish Lords by setting up a tribunal to inquire into the reasons behind the Lords' rebellion and consider the validity of their accusations of adultery and murder. The tribunal opened in October and, on 6 December, the notorious 'casket letters' – eight love letters allegedly written by Mary to Bothwell – were produced as evidence of Mary's adultery and involvement in the plot to murder Darnley. Mary claimed the letters were forgeries and demanded that she be allowed to attend the trial and plead her case in person. Elizabeth refused and Mary's representatives withdrew in protest. In January 1569, the case against her was declared to be 'not proven'. The inconclusive verdict was used to justify Mary's continued imprisonment in England, which meant that she would continue to dominate domestic politics for the next twenty years.

The Ridolfi Plot

Autograph letter written in cipher by Mary, Queen of Scots, to the Duke of Norfolk, suggesting marriage. Tutbury Castle, 31 January 1570.

British Library, Cotton MS Caligula C ii, f. 74

Mine own Lord, I wrote to you before, to know your pleasure if I should seek to make any enterprise. If it please you, I care not for my danger; but I would wish you would seek to do the like; for if you and I could escape both, we should find friends enough, and for your lands I hope they should not be lost, for, being free and honourably bound together, you might make such good offers for the countries and the Queen of England, as they should not refuse. Our fault were not shameful; you have promised to be mine, and I yours. I believe the Queen of England and country should like of it. And you her kept by means of friends, therefore, you have sought your liberty, and satisfaction of your conscience, meaning that you promised me you could not leave me. If you think the danger great, do as you think best, and let me know what you please that I do, for I will ever be for your sake perpetual prisoner, or put my life in peril for your weal and mine. As you please command me, for I will, for all the world, follow your commands, so that you be not in danger for me in so doing. I will either, if I were out, by humble submission, and all my friends were against it, or by other ways, work for our liberties so long as I live. Let me know your mind, and whether you are not offended at me, for I fear you are, seeing that I do hear no news from you. I pray God preserve you, and keep us both from deceitful friends. This last of January. Your own, faithful to death, Queen of Scots, my Norfolk.

The decade following Elizabeth's religious settlement had been peaceful, but when Mary, Queen of Scots, fled to England in 1568, William Cecil immediately recognized the danger she posed to the stability of the realm. His greatest fear was that Mary would become the focus of Catholic conspiracies to overthrow Elizabeth and restore Catholicism in England with Mary as queen. When Mary's trial closed in January 1569 and it became clear that she would remain in England, she was sent to the secure location of Tutbury Castle in Staffordshire and George Talbot, 6th Earl of Shrewsbury, was appointed as her keeper.

In 1569, the plan to marry Mary to a loyal English nobleman was revived in order to neutralize the Scottish Queen's power and resolve the problem of the English succession. Opportunely, the ambitious Thomas Howard, 4th Duke of Norfolk and England's senior peer, was recently widowed and willing to wed Mary. The proposal was supported by a number of leading nobles, including Robert Dudley, Earl of Leicester, whom Elizabeth had previously tried to persuade Mary to marry. This time Mary was far more receptive, believing that marriage to Norfolk would restore her to freedom. However, Norfolk and his allies made the critical mistake of keeping the marriage negotiations secret from Elizabeth, who was furious when she found out and imprisoned Norfolk.

Meanwhile, rumours were spreading of an imminent uprising in the north, planned by two of Norfolk's allies: Thomas Percy, 7th Earl of Northumberland, and Charles Neville, 6th Earl of Westmorland. Both men were members of the disaffected Catholic nobility, who had been excluded from power by Elizabeth's regime, and they had both supported the marriage proposal. The northern earls panicked when they heard of Norfolk's arrest and, despite the fact that their plans were far from complete, on 9 November 1569 launched a rebellion to restore Catholicism in England, free Mary and force Elizabeth to recognize her as heir to the English throne. Some 6,000 men joined the 'Northern Rebellion', but it was doomed to fail, as Elizabeth had already issued orders for Mary to be removed from Tutbury Castle to the safety of Coventry. Faced with the prospect of being outnumbered by the advancing royal armies, the rebels disbanded and the leaders fled to Scotland. Westmorland managed to reach Flanders, but Northumberland was captured by the Scots, returned to the English and executed as a traitor. The Northern Rebellion was the first major uprising of Elizabeth's reign and it left her badly shaken. She ordered savage reprisals to demonstrate that she would not tolerate any rebellion against her authority. It is thought that some 600–800 men were hanged and many gentry were deprived of their estates.

Elizabeth was given further cause for alarm the following spring when Pope Pius V responded, somewhat belatedly, to a request from the rebel earls to excommunicate the Queen. The Pope published his papal bull *Regnans in Excelsis* against Elizabeth, declaring her to be 'the pretended Queen of England' and excommunicating her as a heretic and schismatic. Of greatest concern, however, was the bull's absolution of Elizabeth's Catholic subjects from all allegiance and obedience to their queen. Elizabeth's government responded with a new Treasons Act which introduced tough new laws against Catholics and clamped down on recusants. It also became a treasonable offence to deny Elizabeth's right to the throne, to intend her bodily harm, to levy war against her or to accuse her of being a heretic, schismatic, tyrant or infidel.

The Duke of Norfolk soon fell afoul of the new Treason Act. Following his release from the Tower of London in August 1570, he was drawn into the Ridolfi plot, an international Catholic conspiracy against Elizabeth, which was named after the papal agent Roberto de Ridolfi, who acted as intermediary between the Catholic powers of Europe, English Catholics and Mary, Queen of Scots. The plan was to free Mary, marry her to the Duke of Norfolk and, with Spanish military assistance, depose Elizabeth, install Mary and Norfolk on the throne and restore England to Catholicism. Shown here is one of Mary's secret letters to Norfolk, written in cipher and later decoded by Thomas Phelippes, the government's master forger and cipher secretary. Mary was careful not to write anything incriminating, but her use of the word 'enterprise', which was Catholic code for the overthrow of Elizabeth and her Protestant regime, betrayed her intentions.

The sophisticated network of undercover agents of William Cecil (who Elizabeth made Lord Burghley in 1571) quickly uncovered the details of the Ridolfi plot, and Norfolk and other conspirators were arrested. Norfolk was tried and convicted of high treason in January 1572 and executed on 2 June. For the time being Mary would survive, but she was now thoroughly discredited and would be placed under even greater surveillance.

Madame Si l'extrenité de mon malheur n'euet
esgalé o doleur a ba cause ie ne veuel
vendue insuffisante a toucher p plus
la playe que no cœur souffre Si ne eo
possoble que ie n'i fusse tant publicq a n
Vous visiter par la compagnie que ie vous
fays que ie n'adoure ne peult burne
cerien cay conuen que l'on estre mini
est ce qu'il Vous riste quia autre sor
mais a moy ie ne trouue de coboslat
simo la mort que i'espere nquls
fera bien tost rencontrer Madam
bi Vous pourries voyre la figur
ie no cœur Vous la verrie le po
d'un corps que est Mais ie m
Vous fascheray plus de me ploin
en ayant trop de vostres Il riste ab
que ie Vous aduoue que tou
me bon part de bo meur au Roy
o bo frere et Vous nous abbur
qui ie trouuerie la plus fid
er ie sœur que ia maisu
d ce pour principalle cause que et
Vous apparteennoient de bo goust a
qui ie me istois Je tout digni
que S'il euet en la faueur vous
plays lon que nous cousuis p
er Madam ie nous prie de
limite ensit a la Couetille que
se a part plus ampli
o neces au vostre audrauc
et Crouuis que de l'espaccoplus ayssu
et Se io ns fust vous naturell
l'anyant a qui si mo vostre inceschas
vous le Longu Vu et sœur l'ouer
torte Cobolatio

The Virgin Queen

Autograph letter, written (in French) and signed by Elizabeth I, sending her condolences to Catherine de' Medici, on the death of her son the Duke of Anjou. *c*. July 1584.

British Library, Cotton MS Galba E vi, f. 255

Madame,

If the extremity of my unhappiness had not equalled my grief for his sake and had not rendered me inadequate to touch with pen the wound that my heart suffers, it would not be possible that I would have so forgotten myself as not to have visited you in the company that I make with you in your sorrow, which I assure myself cannot exceed mine; for although you were his mother, yet there remain to you several other children. But for myself, I find no consolation, if it be not death, which I hope will make us soon to meet. Madame, if you were to see the image of my heart, you would see the portrait of a body without a soul. But I will trouble you no longer with my plaints, since you have too many of your own. It remains to me at this point to avow and swear to you that I will turn a good part of my love for him towards the king my good brother and you, assuring you that you will find me the most faithful daughter and sister that ever princes had. And this, for the principal reason that he belonged to you so nearly, he to whom I was entirely dedicated. He to whom, if he had had the divine favour of a longer life, you would have sent more help. Madame, I pray you to give firm credit to this gentleman who will tell you more amply in my stead my thoughts on your behalf. And believe that I will fulfil them faithfully as if I were your daughter born. As God knows, to whom I pray, to give you long life and every consolation.

Your very affectionate sister and cousin,
Elizabeth R.

In the mid-1570s, Queen Elizabeth I remained unmarried and the Earl of Leicester made a final attempt to woo her. In 1575, as part of her annual summer progress through the English countryside, Elizabeth spent three weeks at Kenilworth Castle, Leicester's magnificent stately home in Warwickshire, and enjoyed a series of spectacular entertainments including music, dancing and extravagant firework displays, as well as plays and pageants on the theme of marriage. But, although Elizabeth's heart remained deeply attached to Leicester, she had long since discounted any thoughts of marrying him. Rebuffed, Leicester turned his attentions to Lettice Knollys, dowager Countess of Essex and a close relative of the Queen through the Boleyn line. In September 1578, Leicester and Knollys married secretly. When Elizabeth found out the following year, she raged with fury and banished Knollys from court. Elizabeth eventually forgave Leicester, in 1584, after learning of the death of his young son.

Elizabeth's last serious opportunity to marry presented itself in 1578 in the shape of Francis, Duke of Anjou, the twenty-three-year-old brother of King Henry III of France. The marriage negotiations grew out of diplomatic and political necessity, due to England's growing enmity with Spain, caused by religious differences and a clash of interests in the Netherlands, one of King Philip II's Habsburg territories. In 1572, the Spanish king's attempts to suppress Protestantism in the Netherlands had sparked a revolt against Spanish rule, which quickly spread throughout the country under the rebel leadership of William of Orange. Elizabeth provided the Protestant rebels with unofficial financial support but was unwilling to send military aid, for fear of being drawn into a war against Spain. With Elizabeth refusing to help, William of Orange turned to the Duke of Anjou for support; his willingness to assist the Dutch rebels made Elizabeth and her advisers very nervous about French ambitions in the Netherlands. Against this backdrop, marriage negotiations provided Elizabeth with much-needed French friendship and the opportunity to forge an Anglo-French defensive alliance against Spain. Elizabeth also hoped that marriage to the Duke of Anjou – or at the very least least prolonged negotiations – would buy her time and enable her to hold back Anjou from military intervention in the Netherlands.

In August 1579, Anjou arrived in England to present his suit in marriage, making him the only foreign suitor to court the Queen in person. Elizabeth seemed genuinely enraptured by Anjou, despite his small stature, bandy legs and pock-marked face, and started to refer to him affectionately as her 'frog'. After three weeks of ardent wooing, Anjou returned to France with Elizabeth's agreement to marry him if she could secure the support of her subjects. There was, however, much resistance across the country to the match. Elizabeth's people did not want a French prince any more than they had wanted a Spanish prince, when her sister Mary had married Philip II. Her Protestant subjects were especially horrified by the prospect of their Queen marrying a Catholic prince and the son of Catherine de' Medici, who had ordered the massacre of some 3,000 Protestants in Paris on St Bartholomew's Eve in 1572. Much to Elizabeth's immense frustration, her councillors, who had always urged her to take a husband, would not give her their unanimous support. While Lord Burghley and the Earl of Sussex favoured the union, the Earl of Leicester and Sir Francis Walsingham strongly opposed it, on the grounds that Anjou was a Catholic. Elizabeth was furious but, unlike Mary, decided not to ignore her subjects' hostility to the marriage. In April 1581, a French embassy travelled to London to re-open the negotiations, but Elizabeth explained that she could not defy public opinion by signing a marriage treaty. Her alternative suggestion of a political alliance against Spain was declined by the French king. Anjou and Elizabeth had continued to write amorous letters to each other since first meeting in 1579 and, when Anjou returned to England in October 1581, Elizabeth still appeared to be enthralled. On 22 November, Elizabeth announced to her court that she would marry Anjou after all and gave him her ring, but withdrew her promise the following day after having second thoughts. The following February, Anjou departed England with generous financial aid from Elizabeth for his campaign to help the Dutch rebels in the Netherlands. The two continued to exchange romantic letters until Anjou's death in June 1584, which left the Queen inconsolable. In her letter of condolence, written in French to Anjou's mother Catherine de' Medici, Elizabeth described how her grief had initially rendered her 'inadequate to touch with pen the wound that my heart suffers'. Writing as if she were a grieving widow, Elizabeth claimed that her own sorrow was equal to Catherine's and had left her like 'a body without a soul'.

Madame & dearest Sister ~~I haue receaued~~ youre lettir quhairis by
~~robert carey~~ youre seruand & ambassadoure ~~robert carey, & quhairis~~ ye
youre self of yone unhappy fall as on the one pair
considdering youre rank e sexe, consanguinitie, & longe
fessed goode will to the defunct together with youre ma
& solemne attestationis of youre innocentie I darr n
& wronge you so farre as not to iudge honorablie of your
spotted paire thairin so on the other syde I uishe tha
youre honorable behavioure in all tymes heirafter
fully persuaide the quhole worlde as the same
~~paire thairin, &~~ as for my paire I look e f that y
~~at this tyme quite~~ geue me at this tyme suche
fall ~~satisfaction in all respectis~~ & kynde dealing
~~proofe of youre honorable~~
dis ~~me~~ as sall be a meane to ferenthin & unite en
yle, establishe & maintaine the trea religion, &
me to be as of before I was youre most loue

this bearare
hath sumquhat
to informe you
of in my name
quhom I uerd noe
desyre you to credit
for ye & nou stode him.

The Execution of Mary, Queen of Scots

Autograph draft of an unsigned letter by James VI of Scotland,
to Elizabeth I, replying to her protestations that she had no hand
in 'that miserable accident' of the execution of his mother, Mary, Queen
of Scots. March 1587.

British Library, Additional MS 23240, f. 65

Madam and dearest sister,

*Whereas by your letter and bearer, Robert Carey, your servant and ambassador, ye
purge yourself of your unhappy fact, as on the one part, considering your rank and sex,
consanguinity, and long-professed goodwill to the defunct, together with your many and
solemn attestations of your innocence, I dare not wrong you so far as not to judge honourably
of your unspotted part therein; so on the other side, I wish that your honourable behaviour
in all times hereafter may fully persuade the whole world of the same. And as for my part,
I look that ye will give me at this time such a full satisfaction in all respects as shall be a
mean to strengthen and unite this isle, establish and maintain the true religion, and oblige
me to be as of before I was, your most loving ...*

[Postscript]
This bearer
hath somewhat
to inform you
of in my name,
whom I need not
desire you to credit,
for ye know I love him.

The mid-1580s witnessed growing international tensions, with bloody religious wars raging in both France and the Low Countries. The Catholic plot against Elizabeth I led by Francis Throckmorton in 1583 and the assassination of William of Orange in 1584 made the Queen's government increasingly anxious about international Catholic plots against Elizabeth and her Protestant realm. In response, the Privy Council drew up a Bond of Association for her loyal subjects to pledge to defend her and 'prosecute to death' any 'pretended successor' in whose name an assassination might be made. In March 1585, Elizabeth gave royal assent to an Act for the Surety of the Queen's Royal Person, which established a legal process for trying any claimant to the throne implicated in plots against the Queen. On Elizabeth's insistence, it did not exclude Mary's son, James VI, from the succession unless he was directly involved in treason. After thirty years of refusing to name a successor, this was the first clear signal Elizabeth gave of her preferred heir.

By 1585, after seventeen years of English captivity, James's mother Mary had become increasingly desperate. Now in the keep of Sir Amyas Paulet, who was far less sympathetic than her previous guardian, Sir Ralph Sadler, she was being held under increasingly strict surveillance. Mary had lost all hope of returning to Scotland or inheriting the English throne and James VI had made it clear that he did not wish to take responsibility for his mother or to pay for her upkeep. So, despite having signed the Bond of Association the previous year to demonstrate her loyalty to Elizabeth, Mary took the fateful decision to get involved in yet another plot against the Queen, this time organized by Sir Anthony Babington, a young Catholic gentleman from Derbyshire. Sir Francis Walsingham, Elizabeth's Principal Secretary and 'spymaster', was fully aware of the plot and, with the assistance of his master forger and cipher secretary, Thomas Phelippes, as well as a double-agent by the name of Gilbert Gifford and a local brewer, he was able to intercept and decipher the plotters' encrypted correspondence, which was concealed in beer barrels. On 6 July, Babington sent full details of the plot to Mary, including his plans for her liberation, a foreign invasion and 'the dispatch of the usurper'. Mary's reply to Babington on 17 July, approving his plans, sealed her fate. Phelippes forwarded a copy of the letter to Walsingham and added a small picture of a gallows to its seal.

In September 1586, Babington and his accomplices were convicted of treason and publicly hanged, drawn and quartered. Under the terms of the 1584 Act for the Surety of the Queen's Royal Person, Mary was placed on trial before a special commission at Fotheringhay Castle in Northamptonshire and found guilty of plotting to assassinate Elizabeth. Parliament called for Mary's immediate execution but the prospect filled Elizabeth with horror and she lamented that she and Mary were not 'but as two milkmaids with pails upon our arms'.

Under extreme pressure from her Privy Council, Elizabeth finally published the death sentence against Mary on 4 December 1586. It was greeted in London with bells, bonfires and prayer. James VI wrote to his 'dearest sister' Elizabeth to seek mercy for his mother. It would, he said, be a terrible thing for her to execute someone alike in 'rank and to her sex' and 'touching her nearly in proximity of blood'. But with his sights set firmly on the English throne, James did not go as far as to threaten to break the recent Anglo-Scottish alliance. On 1 February 1587, after much agonizing and procrastination, Elizabeth signed Mary's death warrant but, still hoping that Mary could be quietly dispatched, she instructed her secretary, William Davison, to leave it unsealed. Lord Burghley, however, moved quickly and had the death warrant sealed and conveyed to Fotheringhay before Elizabeth could change her mind. One week later, Elizabeth's most dangerous rival was beheaded.

When Elizabeth was informed of Mary's execution, she was incandescent with rage and insisted that it was a 'thing she never commanded or intended'. Davison was sent to the Tower of London for passing on the death warrant and Lord Burghley was banished from court for weeks. Elizabeth wrote to James VI to apologize for 'that miserable accident' and to protest her innocence. This is James' unsigned draft reply to Elizabeth in which he assures her that given 'your many and solemn attestations of your innocence, I dare not wrong you so far as not to judge honourably of your unspotted part therein'. Then, seizing the opportunity to press his case to be named as Elizabeth's heir, he adds 'I look that ye will give me at this time such a full satisfaction in all respects as shall be a mean to strengthen and unite this isle [and] establish and maintain the true religion'.

My louinge people, I haue bin perswaded by
som, yt ar carefull of my safty, to take heed
how I committed my selfe to armed multitudes for fear of treacherye. Butt I tell you
that I would not desyre to liue to distrust
my faythfull and louinge people. Lett tyrants fear: I haue so behaued my
selfe, yt vnder god I haue placed my
chiefest stringth and safegard in ye loyall
harts and goodwill of my subiects. which
for I am com amounge you, as you see, at this tyme, for
my recreation and pleasure, being resolued
in ye middst and heate of ye battle to
liue and dye amounge you all, to lay
down for my god, and for my kyng-
dom, and for my people, myn honor
and my blood euen in ye dust. I kno
I haue ye body butt of a weake and feeble
woman, butt, I haue ye harte and sto-
mark of a kinge, and of a kynge of
england too. and take foule scorn yt parma or any prince of Europe should dare
to inuade ye borders of my realm:

The Spanish Armada

Original manuscript of the speech delivered by Elizabeth I to her troops, gathered at Tilbury Camp to defend the realm against the Spanish Armada; recorded by the Rev. Dr Lionel Sharpe, chaplain to the Queen's Lieutenant General, the Earl of Leicester. 1588.

British Library, Harley MS 6798, f. 87r–v

My loving people, I have been persuaded by some, that are careful of my safety, to take heed how I committed myself to armed multitudes for fear of treachery. But I tell you, that I would not desire to live to distrust my faithful and loving people. Let tyrants fear, I have so behaved myself, that under God I have placed my chiefest strength and safeguard in the loyal hearts and goodwill of my subjects. Wherefore I am come amongst you at this time, but for my recreation and pleasure, being resolved in the midst and heat of the battle to live and die amongst you all, to lay down for my God, and for my kingdom and for my people mine honour and my blood even in the dust. I know I have the body but of a weak and feeble woman, but I have the heart and stomach of a king, and of a king of England too, and take foul scorn that Parma or any prince of Europe should dare to invade the borders of my realm, to the which, rather than any dishonour shall grow by me, I myself will venture my royal blood, I myself will be your general, judge and rewarder of your virtues in the field. I know that already for your forwardness, you have deserved rewards and crowns and I assure you in the word of a prince, you shall not fail of them. In the meantime, my lieutenant general shall be in my stead, than whom never prince commanded a more noble or worthy subject. Not doubting but by your concord in the camp, and your valour in the field, and your obedience to myself and my general, we shall shortly have a famous victory over these enemies of my God and of my kingdom.

Gathered by one that heard it and was commanded to utter it to the whole army the next day, to send it gathered to the Queen herself.

For almost thirty years, Elizabeth successfully avoided war in Europe, but during the 1580s, a series of events propelled England towards conflict with Spain, which finally erupted in 1588 when Philip II launched the Spanish Armada. Relations between Protestant England and Catholic Spain had been deteriorating for some years. This was due, in part, to the exploits of English privateers (licensed pirates) such as John Hawkins and Francis Drake, who, with Elizabeth's encouragement, plundered Spanish treasure fleets and settlements in the New World. When Drake became the first Englishman to circumnavigate the world in 1580, Philip II viewed it as a hostile act, in direct contravention of the Treaty of Tordesillas of 1494, by which Pope Alexander VI had divided the world between Spain and Portugal, giving them exclusive rights to travel in, trade with and colonize Christopher Columbus' newly claimed territories in the Americas. Philip was determined to protect his vast empire, but Spain had serious economic problems and was essentially bankrupt. His succession to the Portuguese throne in 1580 was therefore a huge stroke of luck, for the vast financial resources of Portugal's trade and overseas empire replenished the Spanish coffers, enabling Philip to support the Catholic conspiracies against Elizabeth in 1583 and 1586 and to start to plan the 'Enterprise of England'.

When William of Orange, leader of the Dutch Protestant rebels, was assassinated in July 1584, Elizabeth's councillors urged her to intervene directly and urgently in the Spanish Netherlands, reminding her of England's likely fate should the Dutch be overcome. For, if Philip succeeded in suppressing the revolt in the Netherlands, it was feared he would use the ports of Flanders and Zeeland as bases from which to launch an invasion of England. The fall of Antwerp in 1585 to the Duke of Parma, Governor of the Spanish Netherlands, compelled Elizabeth to take decisive action. By the Treaty of Nonsuch, she therefore committed English troops to aid the beleaguered Dutch Protestants in their revolt against Spain. To Philip II, this was an open declaration of war and he initiated preparations to invade England. The execution of Mary, Queen of Scots, in 1587 provided further justification for Spain to declare war on England and overthrow its heretical queen and Protestant establishment.

In the spring of 1587, Francis Drake (knighted in 1581) succeeded in forestalling the launch of the Armada when he attacked the Spanish port of

Cadiz and destroyed in excess of thirty ships assembled there. The English boasted that Drake had 'singed the King of Spain's beard', but his actions only succeeded in delaying the Armada by a year. On 19 July 1588, a Spanish fleet, consisting of 124 ships carrying 24,000 men, was sighted off the coast of Cornwall. The plan was for the Armada to make for Dunkirk where it would join up with a 27,000-strong invasion force led by the Duke of Parma, and escort it across the English Channel to invade England. However, the superior and more manoeuvrable English fleet, commanded by Lord Howard of Effingham and Drake, harried the Armada up the Channel. When it anchored at the port of Calais on 28 July to await news of Parma's army, the English seized the advantage by sending fireships loaded with explosives into its midst. Panic ensued and the Spanish cut their anchor cables, causing the Armada to break its formation and become scattered from Calais to Gravelines in the Spanish Netherlands. The next day, the English attacked again and threw the Armada into complete disarray. Defeated, the Spanish attempted to sail northwards around Scotland back to La Coruña in Spain, but encountered severe Atlantic storms. It is thought that about a third of the Armada was shipwrecked off the rocky coasts of Scotland and Ireland and that close to 15,000 men perished.

By 8 August, it was still feared that the Spanish Armada might regroup and attempt another invasion. Elizabeth therefore joined her Lieutenant General, the Earl of Leicester, at Tilbury Camp in Essex to review the troops assembled there to defend the realm. The following day she addressed them, delivering her most celebrated and rousing speech. This is the original manuscript of her words, recorded by Rev. Dr Lionel Sharp, who, as Leicester's chaplain, would have been present when the Queen delivered her defiant oration. Using the full force of her majesty to rally the troops, Elizabeth reminded them of her descent from the great warrior king, Henry VIII, declaring: 'I know I have the body but of a weak and feeble woman, but I have the heart and stomach of a king, and of a king of England too.' As a woman, Elizabeth was unable to lead her troops into battle but, as this manuscript demonstrates, she used her brilliant oratory to help England face its greatest threat for centuries.

Most fayr, most deere, and most excellent
soueraygne. the fyrst sute J make unto yr
Matie upon my arriuall, is thatt yr Matie will
free me from writing to yr of any matter of
busines. my duty shallbe otherwise performed
by aduertising my LL. of yr Maties counsaile of
all thinges heere: and yett my affection nott
wronged It tells me thatt zealous fayth
and humble kindnes are argument enough for
a letter. att my departure J had a restlesse desire
honestly to disingage myself from this french action.
in my absence J conceaue an assured hope to
do somthing thatt shall make me worthy of
the name of yr seruant. att my returne J
will humbly beseach yr Matie thatt no cause
butt a great action of yr owne may draw me
out of yr sight. for the 2 windowes of yr
priuy chamber shallbe the poles of my
sphere. wher, as long as yr Matie will please
to haue me, J am fixed and unmoueable:
when yr thinke thatt heauen to good for me,
J will nott fall like a starr, butt be consumed
like a vapor by the same sun thatt drew
me up to such a heyght. while yr Matie
geues me leaue to say J loue yr my fortune
is as my affection unmatchable. yf euer
yr deny me thatt liberty. yr may end my
lyfe, butt neuer shake my constancy. for were
the sweetes of yr nature turned into the
greatest bittornes thatt cold be. yt is nott
in yr power, (as greatt a Q. as yr are) to

The Earl of Essex

Autograph letter by Robert Devereux, Earl of Essex, to Elizabeth I, pledging his love for her. Dieppe, 18 October 1591.

British Library, Additional MS 74286, f. 33r–v

Most fair, most dear and most excellent sovereign, the first suit I make unto your Majesty upon my arrival, is that your Majesty will free me from writing to you of any matter of business. My duty shall be otherwise performed by advertising my Lords of your Majesty's Council of all things here; and yet my affection not wronged which tells me that zealous faith and humble kindness are argument enough for a letter. At my departure I had a restless desire honestly to disengage myself from this French action. In my absence I conceive an assured hope to do something that shall make me worthy of the name of your servant. At my return I will humbly beseech your Majesty that no cause but a great action of your own may draw me out of your sight. For the two windows of your privy chamber shall be the poles of my sphere where, as long as your Majesty will please to have me, I am fixed and unmovable. When you think that heaven too good for me, I will not fall like a star, but be consumed like a vapour by the same sun that drew me up to such a height. While your Majesty gives me leave to say I love you, my fortune is as my affection, unmatchable. If ever you deny me that liberty you may end my life, but never shake my constancy, for were the sweetness of your nature turned into the greatest bitterness that could be, it is not in your power (as great a Queen as you are) to make me love you less. Therefore, for the honour of your sex, show yourself constant in kindness, for all your other virtues are confessed to be perfect and so I beseech your Majesty receive all wishes of perfect happiness from

*Your Majesty's most humble
faithful and affectionate
servant,
Robert, Essex.*

Dieppe, this 18th October.

Robert Devereux, Earl of Essex, the Earl of Leicester's stepson by Lettice Knollys, first arrived at court in 1587. Elizabeth adored his company and the dashing twenty-two-year-old rapidly became her undisputed favourite at court. At the outset of their relationship one of Essex's servants commented that 'even at night my lord is at cards or one game or another with her, that he cometh not to his own lodging till the birds sing in the morning.' Leicester's patronage and Elizabeth's favour meant that Essex was showered with favours and promotions. In 1587, he replaced his ageing stepfather as Master of the Horse, and he was granted lands and elected a Knight of the Garter. Essex played the game of courtly love to perfection and wanted to serve the Queen, but the gilded confines of court left him restless and yearning for a life of military service and glory. Elizabeth was reluctant to allow her young favourite to leave court but, in 1589, the headstrong Essex defied her wishes and secretly joined an expedition against Spain and Portugal led by Sir Francis Drake and Sir John Norris. Ultimately, the assault in Portugal was a failure and Essex had to return to court to face Elizabeth's wrath.

In 1591, Elizabeth finally allowed Essex to lead an English army into France to assist the Protestant Henry IV against Catholic rebels. This remarkable outpouring of affection, sent by Essex from Dieppe in October 1591, is from an extraordinary collection of forty-three intimate letters written by Essex that chart the course of his relationship with the Queen from 1590 until his death. The letter follows courtly convention of the time; Essex assumes the role of Elizabeth's lover, laments his separation from his royal mistress, and vows that on his return from France 'the two windows of your privy chamber shall be the poles of my sphere where, as long as your Majesty will please to have me, I am fixed and unmovable'. Impetuous and lacking in military experience, Essex made a terrible general. He ignored the advice of others and disregarded Elizabeth's orders with the result that the siege he led ended in failure. On his return to England, however, Essex used his charms to assuage the Queen's anger.

In 1593, Essex was appointed to the Privy Council and he used his new position to promote his views on foreign and military policy, strongly advocating that England should actively pursue war against Spain. Essex hoped to win military renown and set himself up as Elizabeth's next chief adviser, but his political designs led to regular clashes with Robert Cecil, who was the son of Elizabeth's longest-serving minister, Lord Burghley, and Essex' most serious rival for high office. A Spanish attack in Cornwall in July 1595 provided Essex with further opportunity for military action; the following summer, he and Lord Admiral Howard jointly commanded an English expedition to counterattack the Spanish fleet harboured at Cadiz. Essex returned to a hero's welcome in London after conducting a successful raid on the port, but contrary to Elizabeth's clear instructions, he had also captured and burned the town and failed to plunder the Spanish treasure fleet. Elizabeth was furious, but far worse for Essex was the news that Robert Cecil had been appointed Secretary of State in his absence. When the Islands Voyage, which Essex led with Sir Walter Raleigh in 1597, also failed to intercept the Spanish treasure fleet off the Azores, Elizabeth grew disillusioned with her mercurial favourite and, when he contemptuously quarrelled with her about royal policy, he was forced to withdraw from court.

Months later, in an attempt to win back the Queen's favour, Essex offered to lead a military expedition to crush the rebellion of Hugh O'Neill, Earl of Tyrone in Ulster, which presented a serious challenge to English rule in Ireland. Appointed Lord Lieutenant of Ireland, Essex led the largest and best-equipped army ever sent from England but, once again, showed contempt for Elizabeth's orders and instead of making directly for Ulster, headed for Munster where he took Cahir Castle. An angry Elizabeth ordered Essex to march north to fight Tyrone but he concluded an unauthorized truce before abandoning his post to return to England and justify himself to the Queen, famously storming into Elizabeth's bedchamber while she was a state of undress. This time there would be no forgiveness for Essex, who was deprived of his offices and placed under house arrest. Essex was eventually released but now faced financial and political ruin, leaving him angry and humiliated. On 8 February 1601, he rashly gathered 200 supporters and marched through London to raise a revolt against Elizabeth and her Council. Failing to attract popular backing, the revolt quickly fizzled out. Essex was charged with treason and executed on Tower Hill on 25 February 1601.

No 13. 749.

Suche a prelate of the L— shuld be
taught a bitter Lesson than play
be preschuntius and bold apart afor
he k— wi your good Lekyng therof
wiche as I hope is for too your
inttirest So Wyl his Co— of verifi
to mwehi Good Magior toyhis
assevirations at R— Of withe
you hau, or a new b— warnid you
thus you se how to fulfil you
trust reposid — wiche to
from humur unyade I
hau So airly made pacientli
my S— writin and not fraught
w emehin wisidom yit stuffd
w grint good Wyl I hope you
wyl beari w— t i ndistin
hou to Long, w— the kent
sad, as proceding from a hart
that shall euir be fillid w the

Suri affiction of your
Louing and Suri d—
Sistar Elizebe

The Death of Elizabeth I

Autograph letter by Queen Elizabeth, to James VI of Scotland, expressing her pleasure at his willingness to receive advice from her and providing her thoughts on Scotland's diplomatic relations with Spain, France and the Vatican. Whitehall Palace, 6 January 1603.

British Library, Additional MS 18738, ff. 39–40v

My very good brother, it pleaseth me not a little that my true intents, without glosses or guiles, are by you so gratefully taken; for I am nothing of the vile disposition of such as, while their neighbours' houses is, or likely to be a-fire, will not only not help, but not afford them water to quench the same. If any such you have heard of towards me, God grant he remember it not too well for them! For the Archduke: alas, poor man, he mistaketh everybody like himself, (except his bonds) which, without his brother's help, he will soon repent.

I suppose that considering whose apert [open] enemy the King of Spain is, you will not neglect so much your own honour to the world, though you had no particular love to me, as to permit his Ambassador in your land, that so causelessly prosecutes such a Princess as never harmed him; yea, such a one as if his deceased father had been rightly informed did better merit at his hands than any prince on earth ever did to other. For where hath there been an example that any one king hath ever denied so fair a present, as the whole seventeen provinces of the Low Countries? Yea, who not only would not have denied them, but sent a dozen gentlemen to warn him of their sliding from him, with offer of keeping them from the near neighbours' hands, and sent treasure to pay the shaking towns from lapse. – Deserved I such a recompense as many a complot both for my life and kingdom? Ought I not to defend and bereave him of such weapons as might invade myself? He will say, I help Zealand and Holland from his hands. No. If either his father or himself would observe such oath, as the Emperor Charles obliged himself, and so in sequel his son, – I would not have dealt with others' territories; but they hold these by such covenants, as not observing, by their own grants they are no longer bound unto them. But though all this were not unknown to me, yet I cast such right reasons over my shoulder, and regarded their good, and have never defended them in a wicked quarrel; and, had he not mixed that Government, contrary to his own laws, with the rule of Spaniards, all this had not needed.

Now, for the warning the French gave you of Vaison's embassy to you. Methinks, the King, your good brother, hath given you a good caveat, that being a King he supposes by that measure you would deny such offers. And since you will have my counsel, I can hardly believe that, being warned, your own subject shall be suffered to come into your realm, from such a place, to such intent. Such a prelate, if he came, should be taught a better lesson than play so presumptuous and bold a part, afore he know your good liking thereof, which as I hope is far from your intent: so will his coming verify to much good Master Symple's asseverations at Rome, of which you have or now been warned enough.

Thus you see how to fulfil your trust reposed in me, which to infringe I never mind, I have sincerely made patent my sincerity; and though not fraught with much wisdom, yet stuffed with great good will. I hope you will bear with my molesting you too long with my skrating hand, as proceeding from a heart that shall ever be filled with the

sure affection of your
loving and friendly sister,
Elizabeth R.

The 1590s were a difficult decade for Elizabeth I, personally and politically. Despite the English defeat of the Armada in 1588, war with Spain dragged on and threatened further Spanish attempts to conquer England. The assassination of King Henry III of France in 1589 and the accession of the Protestant Henry IV unleashed a bloody civil war, and between1589 and 1591 Elizabeth felt obliged to send troops to support the French king against the Catholic League of France and its ally, Philip II. At the same time, England continued to provide military assistance to the United Provinces of the Netherlands in their fight against Spain. These continental commitments placed Elizabeth, who was always reluctant to go to war, under considerable strain and put England's limited financial resources under enormous pressure. To make matters worse, in 1595, rebellion erupted in Ireland against English attempts to impose direct rule. The rebel forces were led by Hugh O'Neill, Earl of Tyrone, who appealed to Philip II for support, raising the possibility that Spain would invade Ireland and use it as a base from which to attack England. In August 1598, O'Neill's forces inflicted a heavy defeat on an English army at Yellow Ford in Armagh. Eight months later, the Earl of Essex's attempts to suppress Tyrone ended in disaster, and it would be another four years before he was eventually defeated in 1603 by Elizabeth's last Lord Deputy of Ireland, Charles Blount, Lord Mountjoy.

The financial strain of war was worsened by economic recession and high inflation, successive poor harvests, disease and famine, all of which created social instability. Elizabeth also suffered personally, with the loss of a number of her trusted advisers, on whom she had depended for many years. In 1588, less than a month after the defeat of the Armada, the Earl of Leicester, Elizabeth's great love, died. A week before his death, he had written a note to the Queen, requesting a favour. On it, Elizabeth wrote 'his last letter' and she kept it among her most treasured possessions until she died. Leicester was followed to the grave in 1590 by Sir Francis Walsingham, Principal Secretary and 'spymaster'; in 1591 by Sir Christopher Hatton, Lord Chancellor of England and a favourite of Elizabeth's; and in 1596 by Sir Francis Knollys, Treasurer of the Royal Household. Lord Burghley continued to serve the Queen until his death in August 1598, but he became increasingly frail and debilitated and passed many of his responsibilities to his son Robert. Elizabeth was left bereft by the death of Burghley who, from the start of her reign, had been her chief adviser, loyal servant and her 'Spirit', as she herself nicknamed him.

The Queen was ageing too, of course, and the loss of so many close friends and advisers must have made her increasingly aware of her own approaching mortality. Nevertheless, she refused to nominate her successor, even though there was no shortage of contenders for the throne. These included Edward, Lord Beauchamp, great-grandson of Mary Tudor by her marriage to Charles Brandon, Duke of Suffolk, and Arabella Stuart, great-granddaughter of Margaret Tudor by her marriage to the Earl of Angus. The strongest candidate of all, though, was James VI of Scotland, son of Mary, Queen of Scots, and, after Elizabeth, the most senior living descendant of Henry VII. James had the added attractions of being Protestant, a proven ruler, and the father of two sons: Henry, Prince of Wales (who died in 1612), and the future King Charles I.

James and Elizabeth never met, but it was evident that he was the Queen's preferred heir. They had, in fact, been in regular communication since the early 1580s, with Elizabeth frequently providing James with outspoken advice on the craft of monarchy. Incredibly, this particular letter was written by Elizabeth just eleven weeks before her death. In it she responds to James' request for advice on opening diplomatic relations with Spain, which she warns him against, and on how he should deal with Henry IV of France and the Vatican. The elegant italic hand of Elizabeth's youth has been replaced with her virtually illegible 'skrating' hand for which, as here, she often apologized. But Elizabeth's flourished signature is still instantly recognizable, albeit as a much larger and more elaborate version of the one she added to her letter to Edward VI in 1553 (see p.143). Physically, Elizabeth was in decline but her words to James, although written with a tremulous, arthritic hand, still resonate with the same fighting spirit of her famous Armada speech.

Ten days after writing this letter, the Queen caught a severe cold and fell into a steady decline. After an incredible reign of forty-four years, Elizabeth I died on 24 March 1603, bringing to a close a great and glorious era in English history and the rule of the Tudors. As expected, the crown passed to James VI of Scotland, who – as James I – became England's first Stuart monarch and 'King of Great Britain and Ireland'.

Index